Drive and Stroll in

Warwickshire

Angela Jefferies

COUNTRYSIDE BOOKS
NEWBURY BERKSHIRE

First published 2008

COUNTRYSIDE BOOKS
3 Catherine Road
Newbury, Berkshire

To view our complete range of books,
please visit us at
www.countrysidebooks.co.uk

ISBN 978 1 84674 071 8

The cover picture showing
Wolston, supplied by Bill Meadows

Maps by Gelder Design & Mapping
Designed by Peter Davies, Nautilus Design

Produced through MRM Associates Ltd., Reading
Typeset by CJWT Solutions, St Helens
Printed in Thailand

Contents

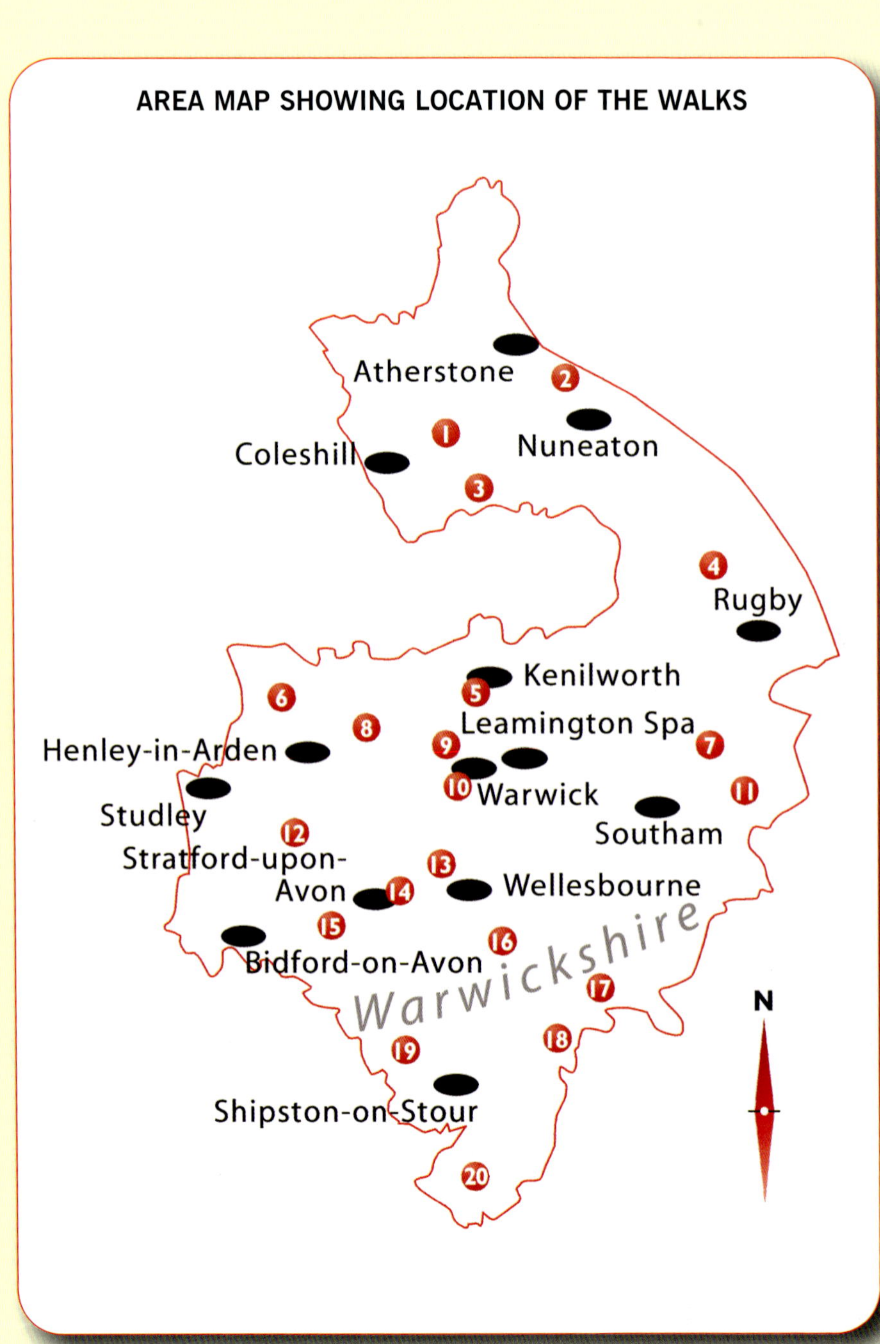
AREA MAP SHOWING LOCATION OF THE WALKS
Atherstone
2
1
Nuneaton
Coleshill
3
4
Rugby
Kenilworth
5
6
8
Leamington Spa
7
Henley-in-Arden
9
10
Warwick
11
Studley
Southam
12
Stratford-upon-Avon
13
14
Wellesbourne
15
16
Bidford-on-Avon
Warwickshire
17
N
18
19
Shipston-on-Stour
20

Contents

PUBLISHER'S NOTE

We hope that you obtain considerable enjoyment from this book; great care has been taken in its preparation. Although at the time of publication all routes followed public rights of way or permitted paths, diversion orders can be made and permissions withdrawn.

We cannot, of course, be held responsible for such diversion orders and any inaccuracies in the text which result from these or any other changes to the routes nor any damage which might result from walkers trespassing on private property. We are anxious though that all details covering the walks are kept up to date and would therefore welcome information from readers which would be relevant to future editions.

The simple sketch maps that accompany the walks in this book are based on notes made by the author whilst checking out the routes on the ground. They are designed to show you how to reach the start, to point out the main features of the overall circuit and they contain a progression of numbers that relate to the paragraphs of the text.

However, for the benefit of a proper map, we do recommend that you purchase the relevant Ordnance Survey sheet covering your walk. The Ordnance Survey maps are widely available, especially through booksellers and local newsagents.

Introduction

Warwickshire is set in the centre of England and is as far from the coast as it is possible to be, yet, what it might lack in coastal or mountain views, it more than makes up for in its pretty, rural, gently undulating countryside. Flatter in the north and becoming hillier as it approaches the northern extremities of the Cotswolds in the south, it has a wide variety of terrain to explore.

The county has much to offer besides Shakespeare, its most famous son. Warwick Castle, the finest medieval castle in England, Kenilworth Castle, a wonderful romantic ruin, stately homes, open countryside with panoramic views, pretty villages and hundreds of miles of public footpaths all conspire to offer the walker a cornucopia of choice.

Almost without exception, the routes in this book are waymarked with the Warwickshire County Council yellow arrows. A number of the walks follow parts of the long-distance footpaths that criss-cross the county: the Heart of England Way, the Arden Way and the Centenary Way. A sketch map accompanies each walk and this, combined with the written directions, should ensure that you stay on the right track. It is advisable, however, to take the relevant Ordnance Survey map with you as well.

I have included advice on suitable places to leave your car while you are walking and, for those occasions when you prefer not to carry a picnic, I have suggested a pub or tearoom on or near the route (and have included a telephone number so that you can check the opening times). Details of places of interest nearby are also given, so that you can extend the outing if you wish.

Warwickshire is my county. I have lived here almost all of my life. I cannot profess to know every little corner, but I have taken great pleasure in describing my favourite walks – and I hope I may even have found some new places for you to visit.

Angela Jefferies

ACKNOWLEDGEMENTS

A warm thank you to the friends who have test walked all of these routes for me, particularly Catharine, who has walked every one, and Trevor, who shared them all with me, and is my companion on the Greatest Trek of All.

1 Shustoke

Shustoke reservoir

Distance 3¾ miles 2 hours
Terrain Mostly level with one gentle descent, on field paths and short distances on country lanes **Map:** OS Explorer 232 (GR 226909)

How to get there

From junction 4 of the M6, follow the A446 towards Coleshill for 2 miles to a roundabout. Take the third exit, the B4114, signed to Coleshill and Shustoke. At the crossroads go straight ahead, still on the B4114, to Shustoke, about 2½ miles. **Parking:** On entering Shustoke, just after the 40 mph signs, turn left into Shustoke reservoir car park.

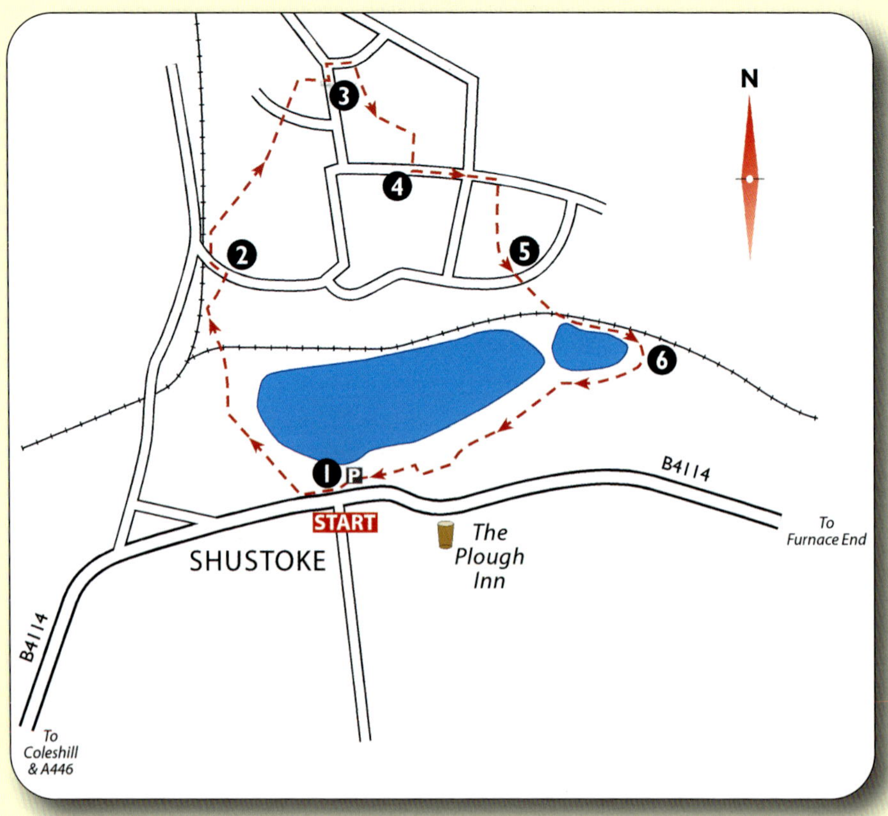

Introduction

The walk goes through some of the prettiest parts of north Warwickshire. There are good views of the area, including the distant West Midlands conurbation, but the circuit is rural all the way, starting and finishing at Shustoke reservoir, which is actually two separate lakes. The larger is the home of a sailing club and the smaller is a wildlife haven. Shustoke is an attractive village. Next to the pub is the pound where, in days gone by, stray animals were kept whilst waiting for their owners to collect them. The route follows the Centenary Way along the reservoir.

Refreshments

The **Plough Inn** at Shustoke is a delightful village pub dating from 1790, where you will receive the warmest of welcomes. A wide choice of food is offered, with an extensive regular menu plus different daily choices. Senior citizens' lunches are available on Monday to Friday, and there is a special menu for Sundays. Serving times are 12 noon to 2 pm and 6 pm to 9 pm during the week; 12 noon to 9 pm on Saturday; 12 noon to 8 pm on Sunday. Telephone: 01675 481557.

THE WALK

Walk back to the main road and turn right to continue along the footpath for 300 yards. Turn right at the entrance to the **Severn Trent Sewage Treatment Works**, and take the footpath to the left of a hedge. Walk along the field with the hedge, then a wire fence, on the right. Keep straight ahead through this field and the next, to a footbridge amongst the trees at the far end. Cross the bridge and walk straight across the next field, aiming for a stile in the wire fence. Cross the stile and follow the path over the railway to a metal stile and walk along the sheltered footpath. Turn right at the '**Colin Teall Wood**' sign, then immediately left, and walk straight ahead, keeping the hedge on the left, to arrive at a wooden stile.

Once over the stile, there is a lane. Turn left and then right almost immediately, just before the railway bridge. The path goes down some wooden steps. Keep straight ahead for 150 yards, with the hedge on the left, to a field corner.

This hedge is home to several species of small birds, including tits and goldfinches.

Go through the gap in the hedge and keep the hedge on the right for 120 yards. Turn right over a wooden footbridge and then left, keeping the hedge on the left. Go straight ahead, and cross another wooden footbridge. After 50 yards, cross the wooden stile into a field. Now walk through the next three fields, passing to the left of a wooden barn, to emerge onto a farm track. Cross the track, go over the stile and across the field, to the right corner by a telegraph pole. The path veers right to a stile in the corner. Cross the stile and the wooden footbridge, and keep ahead to cross two more stiles to reach the road.

Turn left then immediately right into **Deep Lane**. After 80 yards, turn right onto a footpath between houses. The path follows a wooden fence round a garden. At the end of the path go right over a stile and wooden footbridge. Head for a metal gate 80 yards away, which leads into a small field.

The 18th-century Plough Inn

Walk through the field, heading for the top left corner. Cross over the stile. Walk straight ahead for 20 yards to the end of a wooden fence, then turn right at 45° towards a stile near the right end of a wooden fence in the hedge opposite. Cross the stile and the wooden footbridge and, in the next field, keep the hedge on the left to cross a stile in the field corner. The path joins a lane.

 4

Go left on the lane and keep straight ahead. Continue over the road junction and 140 yards further on turn right over a stile to walk along a wide track. Keep straight ahead over two more stiles and then head diagonally for the left corner of the next field. Turn left immediately before two adjacent telegraph poles to go over a wooden footbridge and stile. Turn right along a narrow footpath to cross a stile and emerge onto a country lane.

 5

Turn left on the lane and, in 30 yards, cross another stile into a field.

Now Shustoke reservoir comes into view through the trees. This belongs to Severn Trent Water Authority, and is filled by the River Bourne. It provides water for Nuneaton and the Coventry area and is also a widely-used leisure facility, providing opportunities for sailing and fly fishing.

Go diagonally downhill to the left and over the stile in the bottom corner. In 15 yards cross another stile and then go through the tunnel under the railway. Turn left and walk along a broad path for ¼ mile. The path now joins the circular walk around the reservoir.

Turn right at the 'Circular Walk' sign and follow the footpath, keeping the **River Bourne** on the left as far as the next 'Circular Walk' sign.

Sightings of otters have been reported along the River Bourne.

Turn right through the wooden gate and follow the path alongside the smaller lake. Cross the bridge and go straight ahead to walk along the side of the second lake.

Wild flowers abound along the grassy banks in the summer.

The path goes through a wooden kissing gate, past the **Shustoke Sailing Club** and returns to the car park.

PLACE OF INTEREST NEARBY

Hoar Park Craft Village near Ansley is open all year and is reached via the B4114 east of Shustoke. It comprises a craft, antique and garden centre, a restaurant and a working farm covering 143 acres, including a children's farm. Telephone: 02476 394433.

2 Caldecote

The Coventry Canal

Distance 4 miles 2 hours
Terrain Level; field paths and canal towpath **Map:** OS Explorer 232 (GR 341936)

How to get there

Take the B4114 from Nuneaton towards Atherstone. Continue for 1½ miles and fork right onto the B4111, signed 'Atherstone'. After about 300 yards turn right at a sign to the Community Nature Area. **Parking:** There is a free car park about 100 yards along the lane on the right.

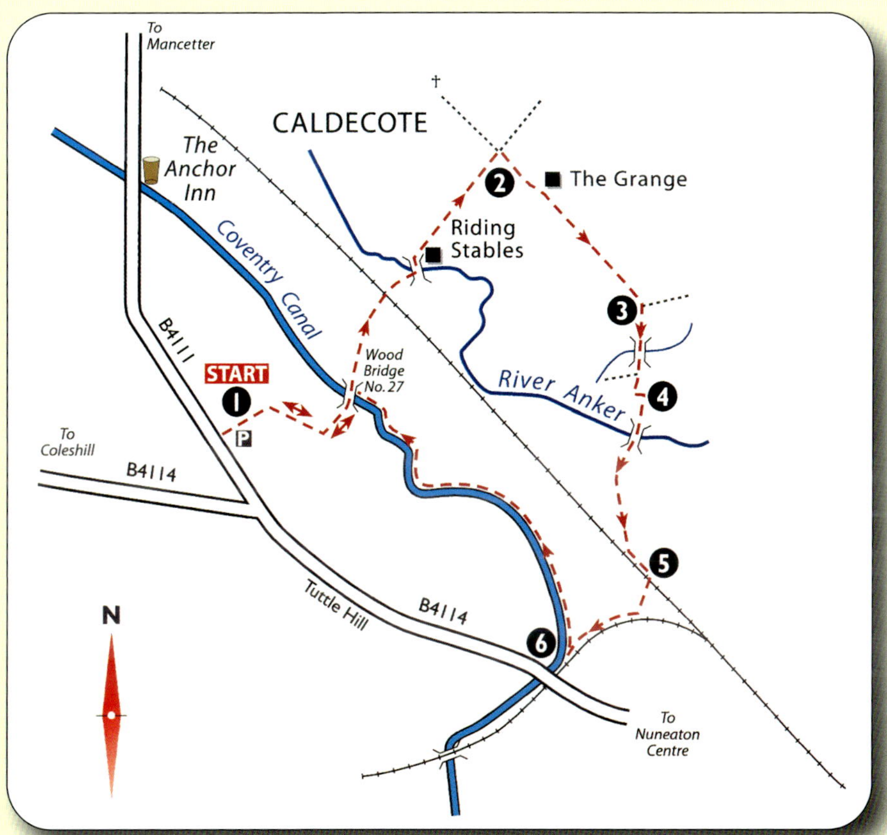

Introduction

Beginning and ending at the Coventry Canal, this walk passes through delightful north Warwickshire countryside, across open farmland, down country tracks and past woodland. The wide-open vistas give a wonderful feeling of space and the quarry works are a reminder of the area's established industrial heritage. Where once quarries and spoil heaps reared their heads, these are now landscaped, and some have become nature reserves and areas for the public to enjoy.

Refreshments

The **Anchor Inn** on Mancetter Road, Hartshill, is just a short drive from the car park. Turn right onto the B4111, and in 1½ miles you will see the Anchor on the right, just over the canal bridge. They are open lunchtimes and evenings at the weekend but only in the evenings Monday to Friday. Telephone: 02476 398839. About a mile past the Anchor on the B4111 is Dobbies Garden World where there is a restaurant serving a wide choice of food and drink to 5 pm each day (4 pm on Sundays). Telephone: 01827 715511.

THE WALK

A nature trail has been laid out over 8 acres, beginning at the car park. There is an information board at the start, showing the route and giving details of what may be seen.

Walk on down the lane from the car park. There are some excellent views across the fields to Leicestershire. Continue down the lane, past the marina entrance, over the canal and straight ahead along a wide track marked 'Public Bridleway'. The path passes under the railway and bends to the left to cross the **River Anker** by a wooden footbridge. There are some riding stables on the right. Continue straight ahead up the lane for about 600 yards where the walk turns right, through a gate by a cattle grid, signed '**The Grange**'.

Caldecote Hall is on the left. It was the home of Colonel Purefoy, a supporter of Oliver Cromwell. In 1642, the Colonel's wife, son-in-law and a small group of staff held out for three days against 500 Royalists, during the Civil War. The original building was destroyed by fire and the present hall was built in 1880. It is privately owned and not open to the public. However, the church may be visited. It was built in the 12th/13th centuries and contains monuments to the Purefoy family.

The next part of the circuit used to be known as 'The Ghost Walk'. It is part of the original route from Caldecote to Weddington. The story goes that in 1832 a young woman used to walk to Weddington Meadows to meet her lover, a married man. But when his wife found out, the husband killed his lover. He was hanged in Warwick two months later.

The first part of this track is tarmacked and is a good walking surface. The path loops round the boundary of **The Grange** and follows a long wooden fence. At the end of the fence you will find yourself in open countryside, on a wide track, with yellow waymarks signing the route. There are fine views across the fields. At the end of the field continue ahead onto the path, following waymarks across an open field.

Almost at the far end, where the

path divides, take the right turn. Continue to the field boundary and cross a stream on a wooden footbridge. Head straight across the open field towards a bridge under the disused railway.

Across the fields to the right, the volcanic-shaped spoil heap from the local quarry stands on the skyline. It is known locally as Mt Jud, after the quarry firm, Judkins.

Do not pass under the bridge, but turn right immediately before it, climb up the steps and turn right onto the disused railway. The route now follows a delightful leafy path for about ½ mile, crossing the infant **River Anker**.

To the left, ridge and furrow fields can be seen. This term describes the pattern of peaks and troughs caused by the system of ploughing in the Middle Ages. Large fields were divided into long, narrow plots, and farmers were given a number of strips to cultivate.

Eventually the path narrows and twists left and right and then leaves the disused railway at a metal stile.

A few yards after the stile, turn right under the mainline railway and walk up the gentle slope. Ignore the footbridge on the left over the branch railway line, but keep this railway line on your left. The path

On the route

bends to the right and continues up the track. Pass over the disused railway, walk past the quarry works gate on the right and turn left, past some cottages, to join the road.

Quarrying here began hundreds of years ago and some of the rocks are more than six hundred million years old. They were formed when ash erupting from a nearby volcano landed in the sea.

Turn right along the road and in a few yards right again to join the canal towpath. Turn right along the towpath. Soon the noise of the road and the quarry works are left behind as the towpath meanders along the lush green corridor. Here life is at a slower pace, the boats cruise tranquilly, fishermen sit hoping for a catch and ramblers are out enjoying the exercise. The canal twists and turns on its way towards Atherstone, and within a mile **Wood Bridge** (no 27) is reached. Leave the canal at this point and walk back up the track to the car park.

The Coventry Canal was built to connect Coventry to the main canal system, and to bring coal to the city from the coalfields of Bedworth. The first part of the canal, from Coventry to Bedworth, was opened in 1769, but, due to financial problems, the connection to the main canal system at Fradley Junction took another 21 years.

PLACES OF INTEREST NEARBY

Nuneaton Museum and Art Gallery in Riversley Park, Nuneaton, contains a reconstruction of George Eliot's London drawing room of 1870 and many of her personal items, as well as displays of local history and art exhibitions. Opening hours: Tuesday to Saturday 10.30 am to 4.30 pm; Sunday 2 pm to 4 pm; Mondays (bank holidays only). Telephone: 02476 350720.

If you are in the area on a bank holiday weekend (Sundays and Mondays only) between Easter and September, **Arbury Hall**, to the south-west of Nuneaton, is well worth a visit. It was built on the site of an Augustinian priory and has been home to the Newdigate family for over 400 years. The hall is open from 2 pm to 5 pm, the gardens from 1.30 pm to 6 pm Telephone: 0871 716 2256.

3 Fillongley

Fillongley Hall is passed on the way

Distance 3¼ miles 🕓 2 hours
Terrain Some gentle gradients, a few uneven field paths and short distances on mainly quiet roads **Map:** OS Explorer 221 (GR 281872)

How to get there

Fillongley lies on the B4098 between Coventry and Tamworth. **Parking:** Turn off by the post office and park in Church Lane.

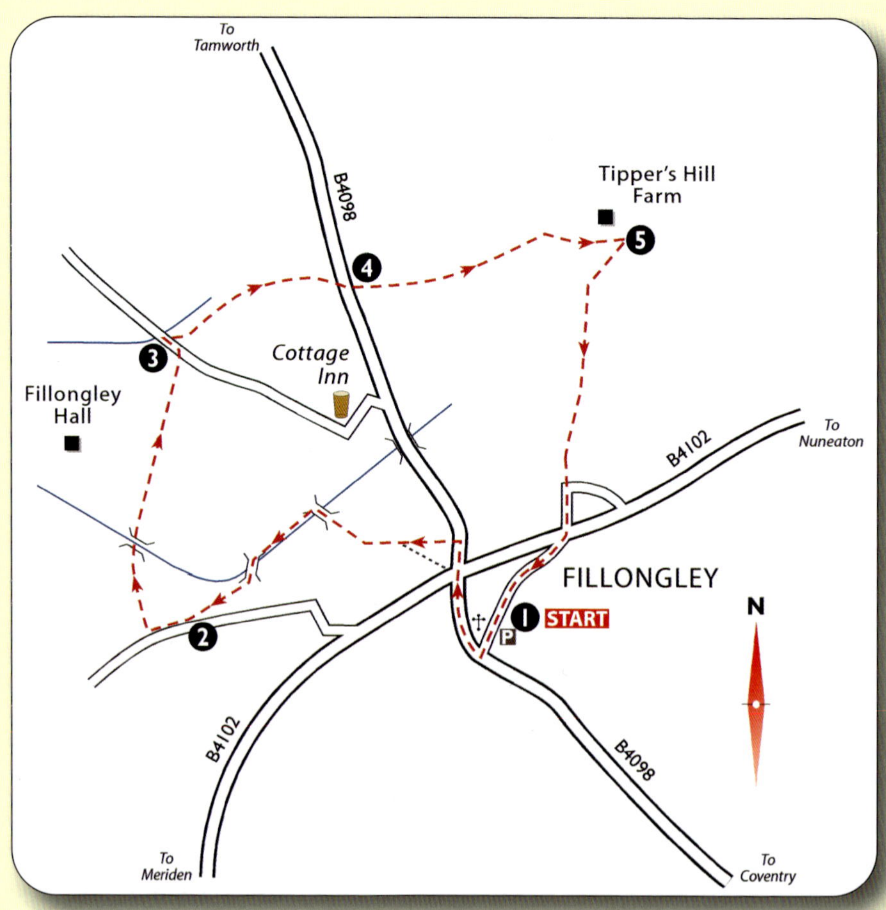

Introduction

This enjoyable walk is mostly on undulating fields in the attractive north Warwickshire countryside. There are some good views along the way and the route passes close to Fillongley Hall. At the end, a short diversion will take the walker to visit the remains of a motte and bailey castle. George Eliot, the novelist, was born 4 miles away, in Arbury.

Refreshments

The **Cottage Inn** in Blackhall Lane, Fillongley is a very friendly pub with a pretty garden overlooking the surrounding countryside. There is an excellent choice of food, including Hawaiian gammon, curry, duck breast and various fish dishes, available every day from 12 noon to 2.30 pm and 6 pm to 9.30 pm. Take the B4098 road from Fillongley towards Tamworth, and turn left onto Blackhall Lane, just after the houses finish. The pub is a short distance along the road. Telephone: 01676 540599.

THE WALK

Walk back to the main road, cross over and turn right towards **Tamworth**. Cross **Meriden Road**, and in 100 yards, look for a metal kissing gate in the hedge, on the left opposite the garage. Keeping the hedge on the right, go over two fields to a metal kissing gate and a stile in the field corner. Turn right and keep the hedge on the right as you make for a metal gate in the field corner. Go through the gate and head straight down the field to cross over a brook. Turn left immediately after the brook and follow it to a gate and a wooden footbridge in the field corner. Cross the water again and keep the hedge on the right to reach a metal kissing gate in the right corner of the field. Turn right onto the farm track and in 20 yards turn left over a footbridge, going up a slope and over a stile. Aim slightly to the left of the nearest telegraph pole, to a stile in the hedge.

Turn right onto **Pump Lane** for 150 yards, and then turn right over a stile by a metal gate, along a farm track.

Fillongley Hall now comes into view, a classic stone building dating from the 19th century. It is the home of the Norton family. George Eliot is known to have stayed at Bede Cottage, adjacent to the hall.

After 150 yards, the track peters out into a field and the footpath continues straight ahead, with the hedge on the right. At the field corner cross the wooden footbridge and the stile into a field. Cross the field to a waymarked stile. **Fillongley Hall** is on the left. Continue on the same line, up the field through a gap in the trees. Pass the cricket field and pavilion on the right, to a metal kissing gate in the hedge.

Turn left onto **Shawbury Lane**. At the road junction take the footpath on the right, just by the sign for **Mill Lane**. Go through the metal kissing gate and head diagonally down to the bottom corner of the field, left of the first telephone pole. Go through the gap in the hedge with a telephone pole on the left. Follow the telephone wires down to the

The church at Fillongley

second telephone pole. Slightly to the left there is a stile in the hedge. Cross the stile and keep straight ahead to the stile in the next hedge. Cross this stile and head to the right of a clump of trees.

There is a distant view of Daw Mill Colliery on the left. It is Britain's biggest coal producer and mines a 16 ft thick seam, nearly 2,500 ft below the surface.

Keeping the wire fence on the right, walk on down to the field corner and cross the stile. Turn right and follow the hedge as it turns to the right and then straightens out, heading for the bottom right corner of the field. You will find there is a gap in the hedge at the very bottom of the field, a few yards from the garage of a house on the right.

This brings you out onto a busy main road, so take care as you emerge and cross it. Turn right and walk along the wide grassy verge for 60 yards, then turn left down a narrow tarmacked road, to **Fillongley Mill**. At the bottom, take the left path and walk through the garden of a house. At the garden wall step over the stone wall stile and turn right. Cross the stream, and walk straight ahead to the top corner of the field, near a pylon. Go through a gap in the hedge. Continue uphill through the next field, and then set a course across the following field for the right of the farm buildings. On reaching the buildings keep them on the left and walk to the end of the buildings. Now set a course left diagonally across the next small field, aiming for the stile in the corner, to the right of the houses.

There are some excellent views from here.

Now, don't cross the stile, but, unusually, turn your back on it and walk ahead with the hedge on your left, so that you are walking at an angle of about 45° to the left of where you came from! This seems odd, but it's what the OS map shows. Go through the gap in the hedge at the end of the field and walk down through the middle of the long field ahead, towards a distant house. Pass through the metal gate and set a course slightly to the left of the hedge, to a metal gate in the wire fence. Go through the gate, along a farm track and through the next metal gate. The track now passes between houses and emerges onto a road. At the first junction keep right and then, where the road meets the main road, cross over into **Church Lane** to return to your parking place.

PLACE OF INTEREST NEARBY

Coventry Transport Museum in Millennium Place, Hales Street, Coventry, houses the largest collection of British road transport in the world. There are cars, cycles, motorbikes and commercial vehicles such as old buses, fire engines and lorries. Open all year from 10 am to 5 pm except 24th, 25th, 26th December. Telephone: 024 7623 4270.

4 Easenhall

The Green at Easenhall

Distance 4 miles 2 hours
Terrain Level **Map:** OS Explorer 222 (GR 464797)

How to get there

Leave Rugby on the A426 towards Lutterworth. In a short distance, turn left onto the B4112. As you approach Harborough Magna, turn left for Easenhall and continue for about 1¼ miles, into the village. **Parking:** This is available on Main Street, or in the car park of the Golden Lion, if you are eating there.

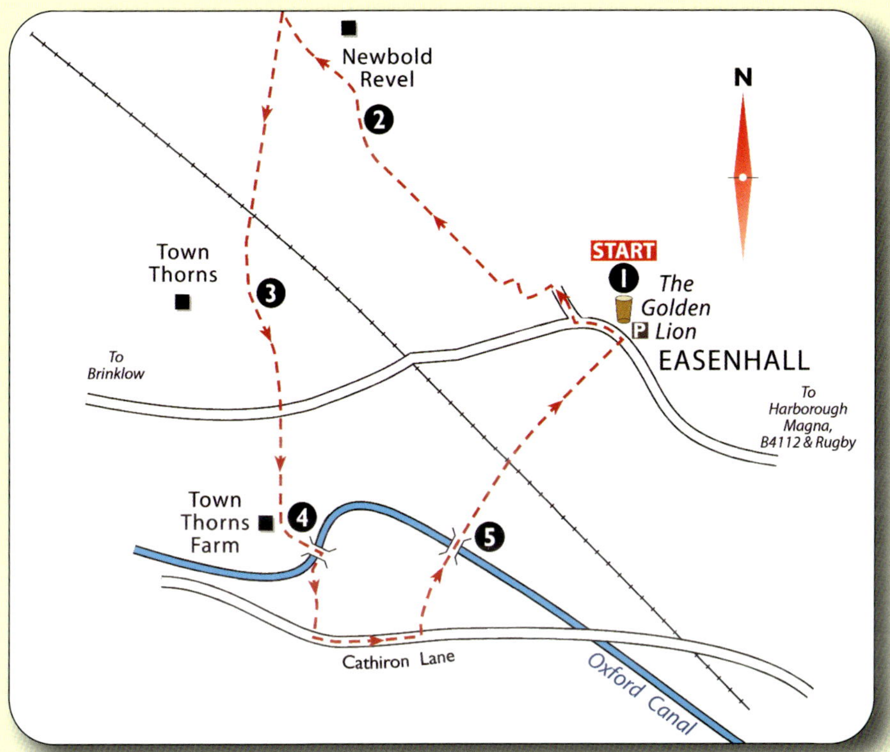

Introduction

This walk passes through broad, wide east Warwickshire. There are wonderful distant views at almost every turn. A feature of the route is the architecture along the way – first the delightful village of Easenhall, an undiscovered backwater with pretty cottages, a listed barn, a village green and a converted chapel built in 1873. The path then crosses fields to Newbold Revel and Town Thorns, both country seats in days gone by. The whole circuit is peaceful and pastoral, well away from traffic noise.

Refreshments

The **Golden Lion** in Easenhall dates from the 16th century and still has an original wattle and daub wall. The menu lists a wide variety of imaginative dishes, including a good choice of fresh fish. Sandwiches, chips and light bites are also available. Food is served every day at lunchtime and on Monday to Saturday evenings. Telephone: 01788 833577.

THE WALK

Walk along **Main Street**, with the pub on the right. Take the right fork at the junction, along **Farm Lane**, signed 'Bridle Road to Stretton-under-Fosse'. After only 100 yards, turn left at the waymarked sign and walk around the perimeter of the cricket field, passing the metal gate, to the diagonally opposite corner. Go through the gap in the fence and right onto a track for 20 yards, then, as the track goes to the right, keep straight ahead onto a path and continue to the waymarked sign, keeping the fence on the right. The path follows the fence as it turns left and, after about 250 yards, the fence and path turn 90° right. After about 50 yards the path and fence turn left, still following the perimeter of the field. The path eventually joins a wide track.

Follow the track to the woods where the path narrows and goes through the trees to emerge in front of **Newbold Revel**.

The path sweeps round to the right and after 300 yards, the college gate is straight ahead, but the path for this walk is on the left opposite the playing field, through a metal gate. At the gate, the path turns left, almost back on itself. **Town Thorns**, a large building, can now be seen on the horizon, and is a good reference point to help with the right direction. Walk across the field towards the railway bridge. At the far end of the field, continue into and across the next field to the bridge, and cross the railway. From the bridge, there is a clear view of the path ahead, and it is also an excellent vantage point for trainspotting on the busy main line. Cross the field, passing under power lines.

At the field boundary there is a stile; cross it and turn left onto the path. **Town Thorns** is now on the right. Walk along the side of a spinney, and turn left and then right at the clearly marked signs. Follow this path through the field up to the right corner, go through a metal gate and cross the track to pass through two more metal gates. The path joins another track. Turn left here and go down to the road. Cross to the other side and follow the track, over the cattle grid and on to **Town Thorns Farm**.

The path goes straight through the farmyard, to a kissing gate, where it turns left and crosses a bridge over the **Oxford Canal**. Follow the track as it turns right and eventually comes out on a road. Turn left along the road for 400 yards, then turn left at the first metal gate, after the brick bridge over a stream. Keep the hedge on the right and pass

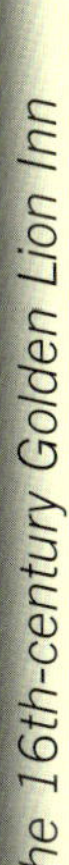
The 16th-century Golden Lion Inn

through a metal kissing gate. Keep ahead and go through another metal kissing gate and over the canal bridge.

Go through the field and cross over the railway bridge. From the top of the bridge, **Easenhall** can be seen directly ahead. The path is waymarked straight across the field to the village. Pass through a kissing gate, and cross the next field as the path goes slightly to the right. The next kissing gate gives access to a short, narrow path between houses, at the end of which is **Main Street**, with the **Golden Lion** to the left.

PLACE OF INTEREST NEARBY

Tours of **Rugby School**, and the museum are available on Mondays, Fridays and Saturdays, starting at 2 pm. Visitors are shown various buildings that represent the history and traditions of the school, including the Chapel, the Old Big School (the original classroom), the Old Gymnasium, the museum and the shop. Telephone: 01788 556169.

5 Kenilworth Castle

The romantic ruins of Kenilworth Castle

Distance 4 miles 2 hours
Terrain Level; field paths and country lanes **Map:** OS Explorer 221 (GR 280721)

How to get there

Kenilworth Castle is well signed as you approach the town, which is reached on the A452 or on the A429 from Coventry. **Parking:** In the main castle car park, the Brays, which is signed from the B4103, almost opposite Castle Laurels Guest House.

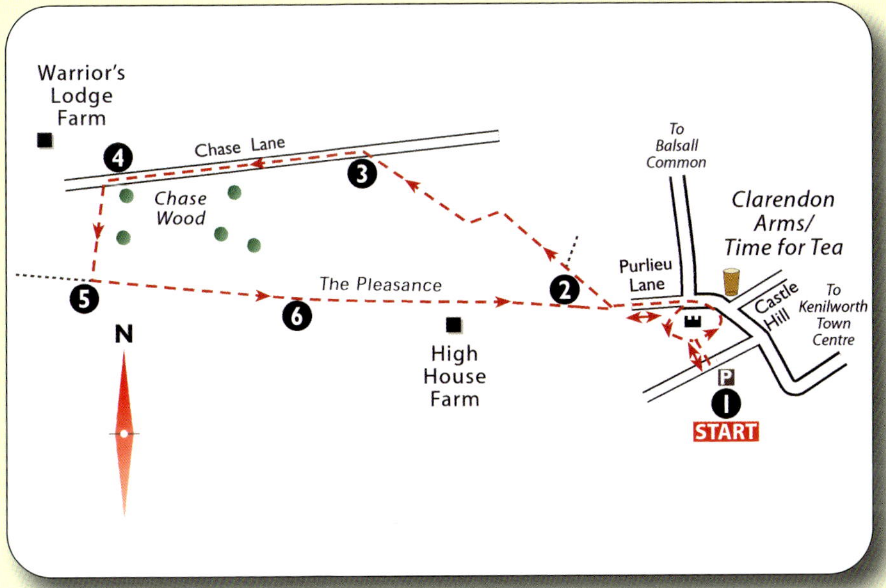

Introduction

Striding out from the romantic ruins of a medieval castle, this walk soon takes you into the beautiful rolling Warwickshire countryside. There are magnificent views of the castle from many points on the route and it looks particularly beautiful late on a summer's evening when its red sandstone walls glow in the setting sun. Skirting pretty Chase Woods, where a rich carpet of bluebells covers the ground in spring, the walk returns across what was once a great man-made lake surrounding the castle. Henry V built a pavilion at the far end of the lake to escape the hustle and bustle of court life – yes, there was stress even in the 15th century!

Refreshments

There are several places to recharge the batteries just a couple of minutes' walk from the Brays car park. The **Clarendon Arms** in Castle Hill serves excellent bar snacks, light bites and sandwiches at lunchtime and in the evenings. Telephone: 01926 852017.

Time For Tea, also in Castle Hill, is a delightful tearoom, offering a good menu from hot lunches to toasted teacakes and afternoon tea. Closed on Mondays. Telephone: 01926 512675.

THE WALK

From the car park, walk past the **castle ticket office** – you do not have to pay – and in about 20 yards go right, down a flight of steps, keeping the perimeter of the castle wall on the left.

Kenilworth Castle is without doubt the finest ruined castle in England. Robert Dudley, Earl of Leicester, spent £60,000 preparing for the visit of Queen Elizabeth I and it must have been a wonderful sight as drums rolled, fireworks blazed and trumpeters fanfared her arrival on a white horse. The Queen stayed for seventeen days, feasting and revelling, and Dudley presented her with new diversions at every turn.

At the kissing gate, keep left. Walk straight across the small car park, making for the top left, where the path continues straight ahead, with the castle wall on the left and a bank on the right. At the next stile keep right, following the garden hedge. In 50 yards turn left through the hedge into **Purlieu Lane**.

Purlieu is an old French word meaning 'the land on the edge of the forest'.

Follow the lane for about 100 yards, passing under telephone wires.

Bear right through a kissing gate, signed 'Chase Lane ¾ mile'. The path now goes up a gentle slope and diagonally across a field. Pause at the top by a ruined barn and turn round to admire the splendid view of the castle. Then take the left path at the fork and follow a clearly defined path across the field. At the kissing gate continue across the next field to a stand of trees. Walk between the trees, go through a kissing gate and keep the hedge on the right for 40 yards, where you will find yet another kissing gate. Go through this and diagonally across the field, heading for the houses on the skyline.

At the far end of the field, opposite the houses, a kissing gate allows access onto **Chase Lane**. Turn left and walk along the lane for about a mile, almost to its very end. The lane takes you past **Chase Wood**.

The origin of the name of Chase Lane is lost in the mists of time, but it almost certainly had a connection with the extensive hunting grounds that used to spread out from the castle.

Do not be put off by the sign that says it is a private road — it *is* a public footpath, but only permitted vehicles are allowed.

Castle Green

 ④

At the end of the wood, there is a turn to the left, just before **Warrior's Lodge Farm**. Take this left turn, and continue along the perimeter of the wood, going down a gentle slope. Eventually the wood is left behind and the path continues to the bottom of the hill, where there is a crossing of footpaths.

 ⑤

Take the left path and follow the hedgerow and ditch on the left. In the spring the banks of the ditch are clothed with an abundance of primroses. The path crosses two fields and arrives at a wooden plank across a stream bed, which is generally dry. Continue on the same line with the hedgerow on the left, crossing a field under some electricity pylon wires to a kissing gate, and now the hedgerow is on the right of the path.

 ⑥

After 200 yards and another kissing gate, **Kenilworth Castle** appears once more on the horizon. Now the path deviates a little from the hedgerow to cross **The Pleasance** and arrive at a wooden kissing gate.

The Pleasance was where Henry V had his hideaway, away from the castle. He called it 'Le Grand Plaisants en Maris', and he could sail here across the Great Mere that used to be here to avoid the pressures of his public life. The bumpy appearance of the field shows evidence of the earthworks that were part of the original design.

Follow the path, which passes through a shaded area with high hedges on each side. The path merges with a farm road, which comes in from the right. Continue towards the castle until you reach **Swan Tower Cottage** on the left. Turn right at the stile opposite the cottage and keep the castle walls on the left all the way round the castle until eventually a wooden kissing gate is reached. Pass through the gate, turn right and go up the steps to the tilt yard. Turn right to return the car park.

The main function of the tilt yard was to act as a narrow causeway, which provided a secure entrance to the castle, guarded by Mortimer's Tower. It was also the place where the knights competed in tournaments.

PLACES OF INTEREST NEARBY

Begun in the 12th century, **Kenilworth Castle** grew over the centuries. It is owned by English Heritage and is open daily throughout the year, except for 24th to 26th December and 1st January. There are often special events, especially at bank holidays. Telephone: 01926 864152.

It is well worth strolling around **Castle Green**, **Castle Hill** and **High Street**, which all have some delightful houses. **Abbey Fields** is a tranquil green oasis in the middle of the town, where the ruins of an Augustinian priory can be seen, founded by Geoffrey de Clinton around 1122.

6 Tanworth-in-Arden

The Doctor's House passed at the beginning of the walk

Distance 3¼ miles 2 hours
Terrain Almost all level, a couple of very gentle slopes, mainly on field paths and tarmac surfaces **Map:** OS Explorer 220 (GR 113705)

How to get there

Tanworth-in-Arden lies to the east of the A435 between Redditch and Birmingham. Approaching from the east, take the A3400 and turn off 1½ miles north of Henley-in-Arden, signed to Tanworth-in-Arden. Follow this road for 4 miles. **Parking:** Park on the road in the village.

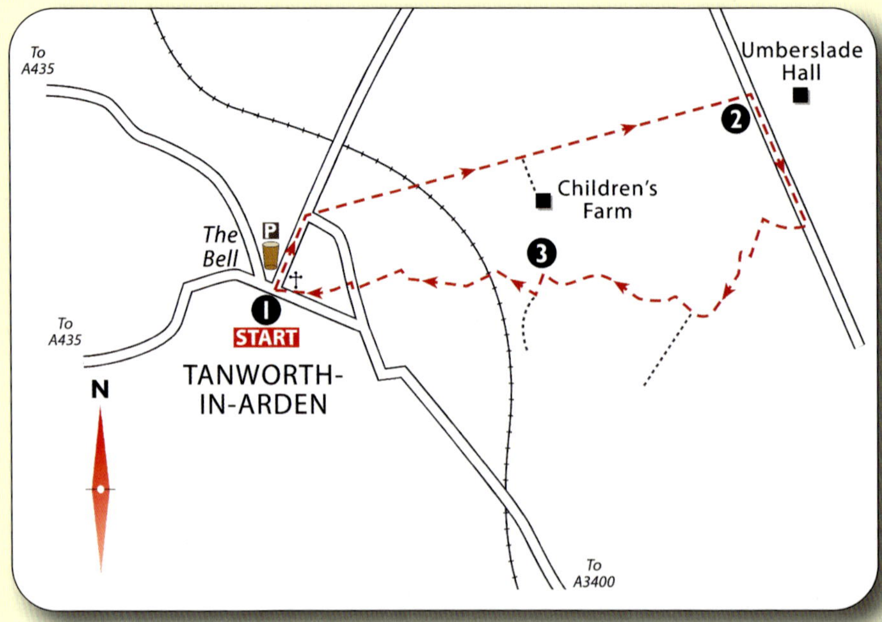

Introduction

Tanworth-in-Arden has all the essentials for a village: a green, a church, a pub, a school and a shop, and is a very attractive place from which to set out on a walk. It was once in the Forest of Arden, a vast woodland which covered half of the original county of Warwickshire. The church dates from the 14th century, but has some modern stained-glass windows. Soon after leaving the village, the walk leads into a mile-long avenue lined with poplar trees. This is the route into Tanworth taken by the Archer family, who originally owned nearby Umberslade Hall. Built around 1680, the hall is now divided into flats. The second half of the walk passes through arable fields and sheep pastures and returns through the village churchyard.

Refreshments

The popular **Bell Inn** situated on The Green in Tanworth-in-Arden offers a good variety of sandwiches, salads, light bites and two course meals at lunchtimes and a wide choice of dishes in the evening, including duck, chicken, steak and fish. Food is served from 12 noon to 2 pm and 6.30 pm to 9 pm on Monday to Saturday and 12 noon to 3 pm on Sunday and Bank Holiday Mondays. Telephone: 01564 742212.

THE WALK

Take the road between the **Bell Inn** and the church and continue for about ¼ mile.

As you walk along this road, look out for the names of the houses, denoting their earlier function – The Doctor's House, Cobbler's Cottage and so on.

Turn right just past **Butts Lane**, to walk along an avenue of poplar trees, signed to **Umberslade Children's Farm**. Follow this tarmac drive, passing under the ornate railway bridge. There is a turn to the right for the farm, but the way lies straight ahead.

Keep straight ahead to go over a stile. The drive now becomes a footpath, and passes through a wooded area. At the end of the wood, the path goes between two columns and along a field to emerge onto a road, opposite **Umberslade Hall**.

Turn right and walk along the road for a little more than ¼ mile.

There are some good views from this road, to Tanworth-in-Arden and beyond.

There is a footpath on the right, opposite **South Lodge Cottage**. Cross the stile by the metal gate and walk across the short field to a stile immediately ahead. Go over this stile and follow the wire fence, keeping it on the right. A hedge soon replaces the wire fence. Continue along with the hedge on the right for 125 yards. Turn right on an unmarked path, immediately before a small plantation. Walk ahead through the trees and cross a stile and a wooden footbridge. Follow the path between tangled trees to eventually reach a stile. Cross the stile into the field and go straight ahead with the field boundary on the left.

After 125 yards, at the field end, pass through the gap and turn right, to follow the field boundary. Keep straight ahead at the path junction* and follow the perimeter of the next field as it turns left and right around a copse. Keep the copse on the right. Eventually it thins out to become a high hedge of trees. At the bottom right edge of the field, go through a metal gate and over a stream. (*From the path junction to the metal gate over the stream is about 600 yards.)

 ③

Turn left and in about 30 yards cross a stile, then go to the left to follow the stream on the left for 100 yards, reaching a large oak tree. Turn right here and walk ahead, passing another oak tree, and a telegraph pole. **Umberslade Children's Farm** is on the right. Continue ahead to a third oak tree and then look for a stile in the

Along the way

corner, about 80 yards away.

Cross the stile and walk through the trees to pass under the railway line. Go over another stile and walk straight ahead across the field to a wooden footbridge in the opposite hedge. Follow the path round the field, keeping the hedge on the left, to another stile in the hedge. Cross the stile, then walk on through the next field and over a stile. Walk along the path to join the road. Turn right for 45 yards and then left, up some stone steps and through a metal kissing gate. Go straight ahead up the field and through the wooden kissing gate. In a few yards, go through the wooden gate into the churchyard.

On the left is the grave of Mike Hailwood and his daughter, killed in a road accident in 1981. Mike was a motorbike racer, winner of nine motorcycle championships in the 1960s.

Follow the path through the churchyard, back to the village centre.

PLACE OF INTEREST NEARBY

Packwood House, a National Trust property, is 2 miles east of Hockley Heath, on the A3400. Renowned for its tapestries and stained glass, the house had connections with the Civil War, and the gardens have a famous collection of yew trees, said to represent Christ preaching the Sermon on the Mount. Telephone: 01564 783294.

7 Broadwell and Leamington Hastings

The Green at Leamington Hastings

Distance 4¾ miles 2½ hours
Terrain Mainly level all the way, on field paths and some country lanes
Map: OS Explorer 222 (GR 438652)

How to get there

The Boat Inn at Birdingbury Bridge, south of Broadwell, is on the A426 between Southam and Dunchurch. Approaching from Southam, follow the signs towards Rugby. After turning onto the A426 travel for 2 miles to reach the Boat Inn on the left. Immediately after the inn, the road crosses the canal. **Parking:** Turn left immediately after the canal bridge into a parking area.

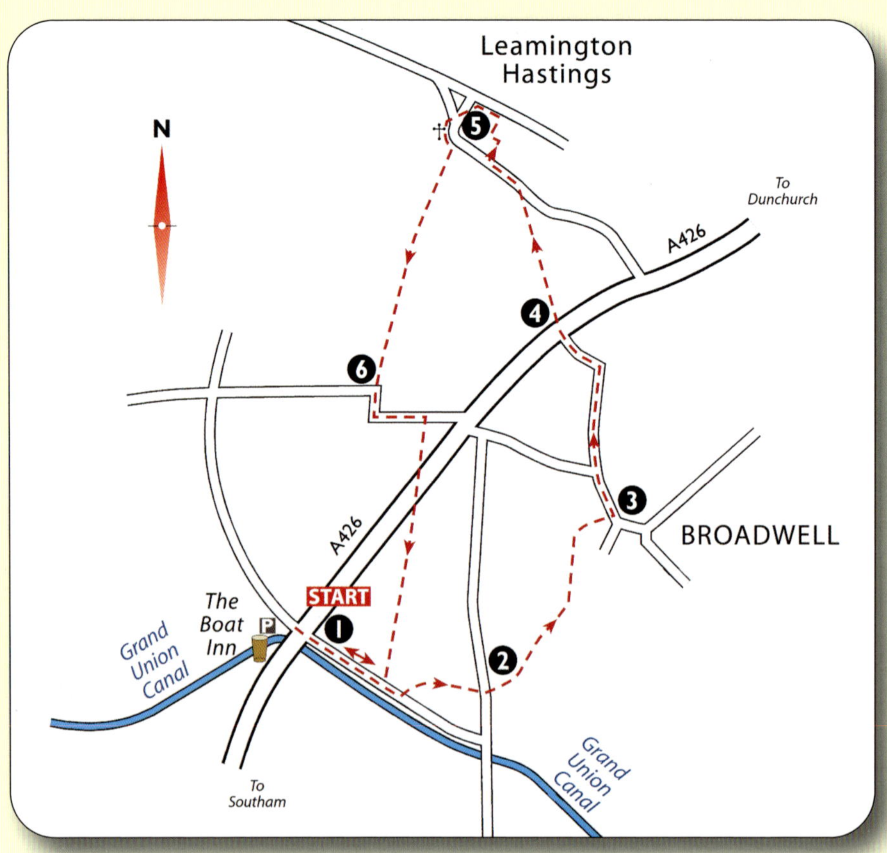

Introduction

This route follows part of the Blue Lias Rings, circular walks linking some of the local villages where Blue Lias clay was quarried. Broadwell and Leamington Hastings are two quiet little communities, well away from main roads, off the beaten track and in the midst of rolling countryside – so typical of this area of Warwickshire. The attractive almshouses in Leamington Hastings date from the 17th century. There is a sense of tranquillity and history as you walk between the two villages on the old way used by local people hundreds of years ago.

Refreshments

The **Boat Inn**, situated at Birdingbury Wharf, provides a good choice of bar snacks. In the bar, there is an attractive mural painted by the well-known canal artist Dusty Miller. Food is available from 12 noon to 2.30 pm and 6 pm to 9.30 pm on Monday to Friday, 12 noon to 9.30 pm on Saturday and 12 noon to 8 pm on Sunday. Telephone: 01926 812349.

THE WALK

From the car park, cross the main road and go straight ahead along the country lane for 550 yards.

The Grand Union Canal runs alongside the lane. It was opened about 1800 and brought coal for the local lime, cement and brick industries. These industries grew up as a result of the presence of Blue Lias.

Pass the first stile on the left and after 45 yards climb the next stile. Turn right and follow the field boundary, keeping the hedge on the right. Walk to the field corner, turn left and follow the hedge for about 180 yards to reach a stile in the hedge on the right. Cross over the stile and go straight ahead with the hedge on the right.

At the end of the field, cross the lane and the stile. Walk across the field, aiming just to the right of the bungalow. There is a waymarked metal farm gate set in a metal fence. Cross the low fence on the right of the gate and walk diagonally through the small field and over the stile. Keep on the same line to cross the next field diagonally to a low fence by a gate. Maintain the same line, crossing the next field diagonally right under the telegraph wires, to arrive at a double stile to the right of a small metal gate. Cross the double stile and turn left, keeping the hedge on the left. Walk straight ahead towards the houses, crossing a stile. Continue for 100 yards and turn left through a field gate, then go immediately right, keeping the hedge on the right. Head for the metal gate between the houses and pass through it to arrive at **Broadwell village green**. Turn right over the small bridge by the gate and cross the green diagonally left to reach a lane by a post box. Turn right to the T-junction by the village hall, and then turn left.

Walk past the **Methodist church** on the left and the **Church of the Good Shepherd** on the right, then leave the road as it bends to the left, keeping straight ahead through a metal gate. Follow the wide track to the left of some farm buildings. After 300 yards pass through the metal gate, ignoring a public footpath to the right, and follow this track all the way to the main road.

All Saints' church in Leamington Hastings

Cross the busy main road with care and climb the stile in the hedgerow opposite. Continue ahead across the field for 200 yards, keeping the hedge on the right. Cross the stile in the corner and take the left of the two waymarked paths. Keep ahead, with the hedge close on the right, to the end of the field, and then pass through a wooden gate into a narrow path between hedges in a wooded glade.

This is the old road between Broadwell and Leamington Hastings, and the wooded glade is part of a private project to establish an English oak/ash wood, on the site of an old sheep pasture.

Cross the stile at the end of the glade and follow the path as it bears diagonally left across the field to the corner. Take the right stile into the lane, then turn left and walk towards **Leamington Hastings**. Just before the Leamington Hastings sign, look for a stile in the hedge on the right. Climb over it and cross the field, bearing slightly left, to reach a metal gate near the left corner of the field. Pass through the gate and in 50 yards cross the stile by the gate onto a tarmac road. Turn left into the village and walk to the road junction.

Turn left at the junction and pass the church on the right.

The attractive All Saints' church, built mostly in the 13th century, is well worth a visit.

Just after passing the church, where the road bends left, keep straight ahead along a gravelled track.

On the left are almshouses built in 1633. They are built of the local Blue Lias stone.

The path passes a barn on the right. After 100 yards, go through a metal gate. Where the track goes to the right, keep straight ahead with the hedge on the left. Maintain the same line through three fields to arrive at a country lane.

Turn left and walk along the lane. After about 400 yards look for a stile on the right, under an oak tree. Cross the stile and walk straight ahead, keeping the hedge on the left. The path goes gently downhill to a stile in the hedgerow. Cross the stile to emerge onto a busy main road. Cross with care and climb the stile on the other side of the road, slightly to the right. Once over the stile turn right and follow the hedgerow to the corner of the field, by a pond.

Dragonflies dart here in the summer and this is a pleasant spot to pause awhile and catch one's breath.

There is a stile in the corner, and a crossroads of footpaths. Keep straight ahead, with the hedge on the right. The path now goes across stiles and fields for about 700 yards, with the hedge on the right, to arrive at a country lane. Turn right and return to the car park. (If you prefer, you can walk back alongside the canal, which is parallel to the lane, on the other side of the hedge.)

PLACE OF INTEREST NEARBY

Draycote Water is about 3 miles north of the parking place, along the A426 towards Rugby. There is a 5-mile perimeter road around the reservoir, a hilltop car park with excellent views and footpaths to waterside picnic areas, a teashop, bird hides, wetlands, nature trails and fishing. The visitor centre is open every day (except Christmas Day) from 7.30 am to 8 pm. Admission is free (but there is a charge for parking). Telephone: 01788 811107.

8 Lowsonford

The Stratford-upon-Avon Canal

Distance 3½ miles 🕑 2 hours
Terrain Mainly level with a few gentle rises; field paths and country lanes
Map: OS Explorer 220 (GR 188677)

How to get there

Lowsonford is situated to the north-west of Warwick between the A3400 and the A4189. Approaching from Warwick, take the A4177 towards Birmingham. After approximately 2½ miles fork left onto the B4439 towards Hockley Heath. In 2 miles turn left, signed to Shrewley, and after about 200 yards turn left again. Go through Shrewley village and turn right immediately after crossing the M40, signed to Lowsonford. **Parking:** On entering the village, park in the lay-by, directly behind the 30 mph sign.

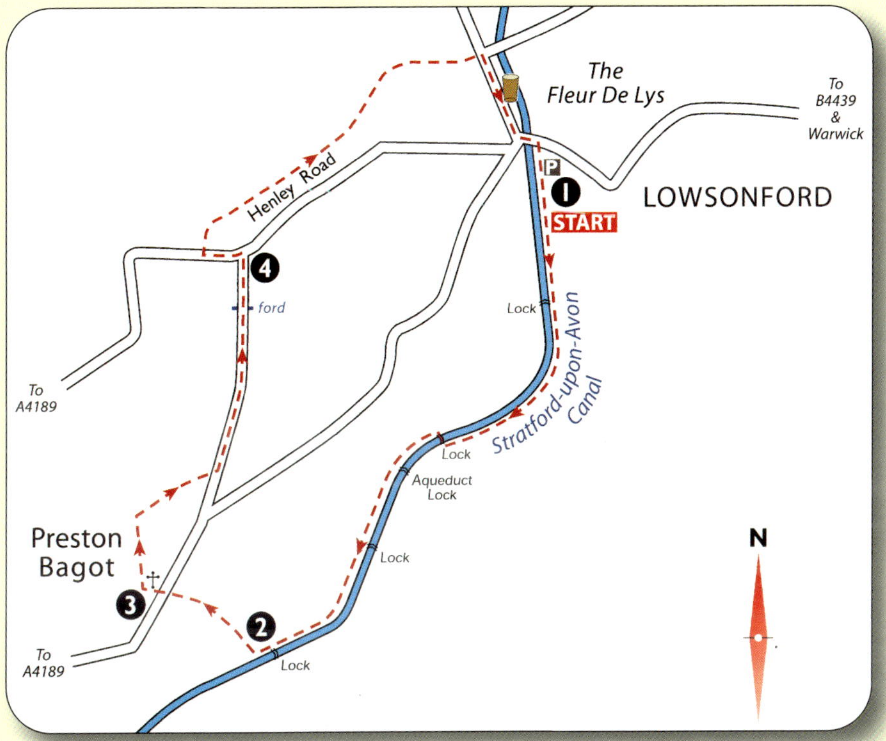

Introduction

The walk begins in the village of Lowsonford – said to be a corruption of 'Lonesomeford'. The first 1½ miles of the circuit follow the Stratford-upon-Avon Canal. In 1958 this delightful waterway was derelict and about to be abandoned by order of Parliament, when the National Trust stepped in and saved it for future generations to enjoy. Now it is a rural idyll, passing through picturesque south Warwickshire. The second part of the walk goes over fields and along bridlepaths and, although lacking the far-reaching views of some of the other locations in this book, the countryside is attractive and peaceful. The route passes Preston Bagot church, a pretty building set in a field, dating from the 12th century.

Refreshments

The **Fleur de Lys Inn** in Lowsonford started serving home-made pies over forty years ago – an innovation at a time when pub food often meant just crisps or salted peanuts – and the tradition is kept alive with a wide choice of excellent pies, still cooked on the premises. There is also an extensive range of other dishes, including daily specials. Food is served from 12 noon to 9 pm on Sunday to Thursday and 12 noon to 10 pm on Friday and Saturday. Telephone: 01564 782431.

THE WALK

Immediately past the lay-by, a gate on the left leads onto the canal towpath. Turn left and walk along the towpath. At the second lock, the towpath changes to the other side of the canal.

Note the aqueduct, immediately before the next lock. There is a good information board here, giving details of the aqueduct, and also explaining about the barrel-roofed lock-keepers' cottages unique to the Stratford-upon-Avon Canal. At the Aqueduct Lock, also known as Bucket Lock, you will see a good example of one of these cottages.

Continue along the canal for ½ mile and at the second lock after the Aqueduct Lock, number 36, turn right onto a footpath.

Follow the footpath over a footbridge, through a metal gate and into a field. Cross over the field to a gap in the hedge, but turn right BEFORE the gap to walk up the hill with the hedge on the left. Go through the gap in the top left corner, and straight ahead to the metal kissing gate in the hedge opposite.

The path emerges onto a lane. Turn right and immediately left, up the concrete drive. Go through a metal gate, and walk alongside the fence with **Preston Bagot church** on the right. Walk to the end of the fence, turn right and keep ahead to pass through a wooden kissing gate. Keep straight ahead, with the hedge on the left, through a wooden gate and onto a concrete path. Walk straight ahead to a metal gate. Go through the gate and walk alongside a paddock to a wooden gate ahead.

Turn right immediately before the wooden gate. The path passes the paddock fence on the right and a hedge on the left. Cross the stile and follow the hedge on the left to a stile on the right of a house. Turn left onto the unclassified lane and follow it for a little over ½ mile. There is a ford close to the far end, but there is a high pavement to cross it.

At the end of the lane, turn left

onto the road and in 150 yards turn right, over a stile, and go straight ahead onto a footpath. Cross the field, with the hedge on the right, and go through a gap at the edge of the copse. Walk through the copse, and 20 yards after emerging into the field cross a stile in the hedge on the right. Bear left at 45° to another stile in the hedge. Cross over the wooden footbridge and set a course at roughly 45° to where the hedge moves into the field. Look for the waymark sign at the field corner.

The lock-keeper's cottage at Lowsonford

Go over the footbridge, walk through a short field with the hedge on the left, and then enter a copse on a wooded path. This eventually emerges by a stile and a metal gate. Cross the stile and walk straight ahead down the field, following the line of telegraph poles. Go over the next stile and across the field, aiming for the left side of a brick built house. Cross the stile and turn left onto a tarmac drive. Follow the drive down to the road and turn right. Walk past the **Fleur de Lys Inn** to return to the parking place.

PLACE OF INTEREST NEARBY

Baddesley Clinton, which dates from the 15th century, is located to the north-east of Lowsonford and can be reached from the A4141 Warwick–Birmingham road at Chadwick End. A National Trust property, this is a small-scale house, where you can feel at home and relate to the people who lived there. The priest holes are a reminder of the persecution of the Catholic church. There is a good tearoom in a lovely old barn. Telephone for details of opening times: 01564 783294.

9 Hatton

The Hatton flight of locks

Distance 4½ miles 2½ hours
Terrain A couple of very gentle slopes; towpath, country lanes and field paths **Map:** OS Explorer 221 (GR 243669)

How to get there

Hatton is 2 miles north-west of Warwick on the A4177 Birmingham road. Turn off on Hatton Hill, at the sign for Hatton Heritage Skills Centre. **Parking:** In the car park (fee payable).

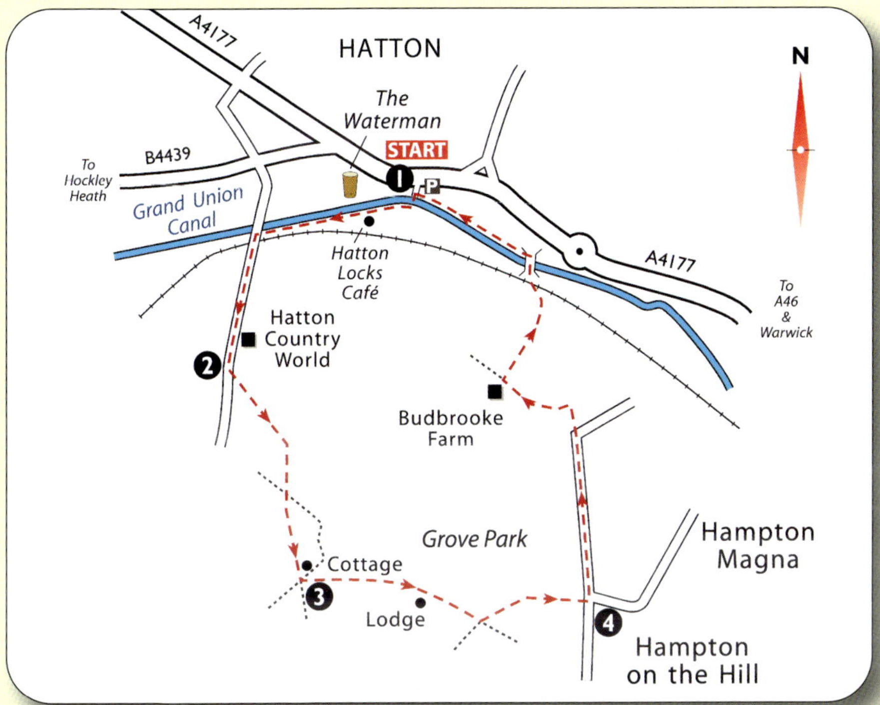

Introduction

At the beginning this walk passes the top four of the Hatton flight of locks on the Grand Union Canal, near Warwick, and, at the end returns along the canal, past more of the locks. A short distance above the top lock, the path leaves the canal and strikes across open country with good views of the surrounding countryside and of Warwick town, with its castle. St Mary's church rises majestically over it all, and is a landmark for miles. The path goes through the grounds of Grove Park, a small country estate owned by the Dormer family. The original house was demolished and replaced by a modern building where the family still lives. A particular feature of this walk is that there are no stiles, only gates.

Refreshments

Just by the car park, the **Waterman** pub offers a wide choice of bar snacks and meals every day, lunchtimes and evenings. This is a delightful old inn, situated on the bank above the Grand Union Canal. There is a garden overlooking the waterway for summer days, and the interior is warm and cosy with low beams and a good atmosphere. Telephone: 01926 492427.

THE WALK

The Hatton Heritage Skills Centre was founded by British Waterways in 2001 to address the need for workers with skills in conservation. It provides conservation training and craft skills for British Waterways staff and other interested groups.

From the car park, cross the canal bridge and turn right onto the canal towpath. The **Hatton Locks Café** is on the left, just before the top lock.

The Hatton flight of 21 locks, stretching up Hatton Hill, lifts canal boats 146 ft 6 ins. It is a daunting sight as it rises ahead. The old working boat people would have made their way through here on a regular basis with their cargoes between Birmingham and London. It takes at least two hours of non-stop winding, gate opening and lock emptying to complete.

Continue along the towpath to the next bridge. Walk under the bridge and then turn left to reach the road. Turn right onto the road and over the railway bridge, passing **Hatton Country World** on the left.

Some 300 yards after Hatton Country World, turn left through a gate onto a public footpath. Turn right along a wide grassy track, initially through woods, then over a field, with the hedge on the right, to the field corner. Go through the gap and diagonally right across the next field to the corner. Turn left, over the cattle grid, and follow the wide track to the next cattle grid. Stay on the track to a third cattle grid by a cottage.

Turn left at the cottage and walk along the same wide track for about 550 yards, where the track joins a tarmac lane. Continue in the same direction along the lane to pass a lodge on the right.

The lodge is one of the original lodges to the Grove Park estate. Just after the lodge is the entrance to the new house of the Dormer family. Warwick Castle and St Mary's church in Warwick can be seen in the distance, diagonally left.

Some 400 yards after the lodge, turn left through the hedge and go through a metal kissing gate in the hedge. Walk straight ahead, with the field boundary on the left. Follow the hedge as it turns right at the corner of the field all the way round the field to where

One of the metal sculptures at the Hatton Heritage Centre

the left hedge ends and a hedge on the right begins. Keep the hedge on the right and go straight along the wide track, through a metal kissing gate and onto the road.

Turn left along the road, signed '**Budbrooke**'. After a little less than ¾ mile, where the road turns right, keep straight ahead on a wide track, to **Budbrooke Farm**. Follow the track as it bends round farm buildings, and, at the end of the buildings, turn right, through a gap by a metal gate. Keep straight ahead down a grass track, through a gap in the hedge and across a field, aiming for a gate by a tunnel under the railway line at the other end of the field.

Pass under the railway and follow the path through the woods to a bridge over the canal. Turn left over the bridge down to the canal towpath and turn right along the canal towpath, with the canal on the left, as far as the next canal bridge and the car park.

PLACE OF INTEREST NEARBY

Hatton Country World in Dark Lane, Hatton, includes a shopping village with 25 craft and speciality shops, a farmhouse restaurant and a coffee shop. There is also a children's farm with a guinea pig village, animals, including alpacas, and a play area. Open daily (except for Christmas Day and Boxing Day). Telephone: 01926 843411.

10 Historic Warwick

Lord Leycester Hospital

Distance 3 miles 2 hours
Terrain Level, on pavements and tarmac paths **Map:** OS Explorer 221 (GR 286649)

How to get there

Leave the M40 at junction 15 and take the A429 to Warwick town centre. Follow this road up the hill past Westgate, into the town centre as far as Eastgate, and a set of traffic lights. Turn right, signed 'Banbury A425'. **Parking:** Follow the road down the hill, keep straight ahead at the roundabout and then take the first left into St Nicholas' Park car park (pay & display).

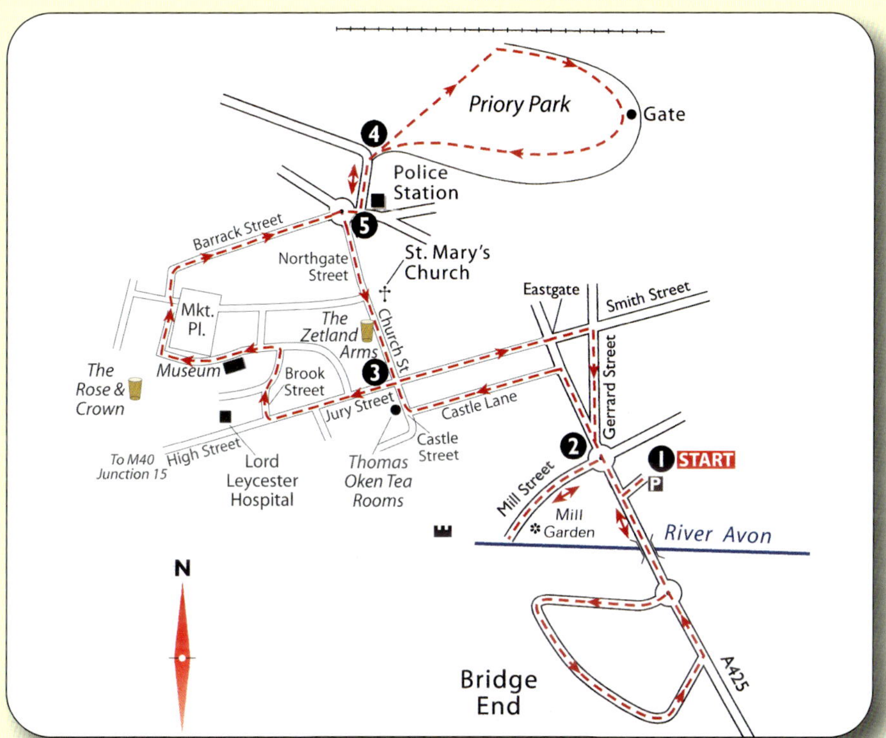

Introduction

There is so much to see in Warwick. This perambulation is but a taster, and you will need to visit the county town more than once to explore all of the places you will pass today, and the many more this route has had to miss! The Great Fire of 1694 destroyed much of the town centre, as most of the buildings were half-timbered and thatched. It is fortunate that the new properties built to replace those lost were built in the early part of the 18th century when the style was for elegant houses. As you follow this walk, every step will reveal new pleasures and surprises, too numerous to mention. The circuit can be completed in a couple of hours, but I urge you to allow much more time, so that you can stand and stare; even a full day is insufficient to enjoy the new discoveries you will make at every turn.

Refreshments

There is a wonderful variety of eating establishments in the town, and the walk passes many of them, including the **Thomas Oken Tea Rooms**, 20 Castle Street, This is housed in a perfect half-timbered building, dating from around 1600 and built by Thomas Oken, the town's greatest benefactor. It has an excellent choice of teas, along with sandwiches, baguettes and delicious cakes. Open every day from 10 am to 5.30 pm (6 pm at weekends). Telephone: 01926 499307.

The **Zetland Arms** in Church Street is a well presented old pub offering a good choice of food, including hot dishes, baguettes and sandwiches. If you get a chance, sit in the garden at the back and drink in the views of all the varied roof lines of the surrounding houses. Food is served from 12 noon to 3 pm on Monday to Thursday and 12 noon to 6 pm on Friday to Sunday. There is no food served in the evenings. Telephone: 01926 491974.

THE WALK

Leaving the car park, walk back to the main **Banbury Road**, cross over and turn left. Walk up to the bridge over the **River Avon**, and pause to enjoy one of the best views in England, **Warwick Castle** with the River Avon at its foot.

This is the finest medieval castle in England, and only a full day's visit can do it justice. Dating at least from 1068, when William the Conqueror built a motte and bailey, it has been added to and adapted over the centuries, to serve the needs of the day. Walls, portcullises and towers were constructed to fortify the castle and later, when life became more peaceful, sophisticated state rooms were added for entertaining .

Continue to the next traffic island, and turn right into **Bridge End**, a delightful backwater, across the river from the castle.

Look out for Broome Place, built in the 15th century.

Continue round until **Banbury Road** is regained at the far end. Turn left here and retrace your steps to the roundabout. Continue over the Castle Bridge, to another traffic roundabout. Turn left here, down **Mill Street**.

Mill Street was not affected by the fire in 1694, and has some magnificent original buildings. At the far end is the Mill Garden – do try to find time to go in. There is a small entrance fee, to benefit charities, and then you are in the most exquisite small garden, nestled under the castle walls, right on the Avon.
There are secret bowers, the original town stocks and a plentiful supply of seats and benches.

Bridge End

Return to the top of **Mill Street**, turn left, casting a glance through the archway to the dark and impressive entrance to **Warwick Castle** cut through the bedrock. Continue up **Castle Hill**. After about 200 yards, turn left into **Castle Lane**, and follow the castle wall until the road turns left. Turn right here, at the **Thomas Oken Tea Rooms**. Continue up to the junction of Castle Street and Jury Street.

Turn left and follow the road down towards **Westgate**, about 500 yards away.

Here you can see The Lord Leycester Hospital, founded in 1571 by Robert, Earl of Leycester as an almshouse for old soldiers, and still used for the same purpose today.

There is a right turn just before the **Lord Leycester Hospital** called **Brook Street**. Walk along Brook Street, pass the end of **Puckering's Lane**, and turn left at the top. Pass to the left of the **County Museum**, originally the Market Hall and walk to the right of Woolworth's, to the **Rose and Crown**. Turn right immediately in front of the pub and walk down this last remaining section of the original road into the town from the north. At the end, go up the steps on the right and cross the road to walk along **Barrack Street**.

Look carefully as you pass the Methodist church hall. There is a ring set into the wall on each side of the road. Nowadays they have merely historical significance, but in days gone by, a rope was stretched across the road to keep back the crowds at public hangings. At the end of the road is a door to an old prison cell.

At the end of Barrack Street, where there is a roundabout, cross diagonally to go down **Cape Road**, at the left side of the **police station**.

After about 100 yards, where the road bends left, walk straight ahead, and follow the tarmac drive to the bottom. Immediately before the railway bridge, turn right into **Priory Park**, a delightful green oasis in the middle of the town. Follow the path to the far side of the park, where there is a metal five-bar gate. Turn right before the gate and follow the path back up the park as it meanders gently up and over the brow of the hill, to rejoin the tarmac drive. Turn left onto the lane and go back up **Cape Road** to the roundabout.

At the roundabout, cross over to **Northgate Street**, and walk along to **St Mary's church**, passing under the arch to walk down **Church Street**, passing the **Zetland Arms** on the way. At the junction, turn left, and walk down **Jury Street** to the traffic lights. Go straight across, under **Eastgate** and passing the birthplace of Walter Savage Landor, a 19th-century poet, on the left. After a few yards, turn right into **Gerrard Street**. Continue to the end of the street, cross the road and take the path to the left of the church through the churchyard to return to the car park.

PLACES OF INTEREST NEARBY

Warwick Castle really needs a full day to do it justice. Open daily except 25th December. Admission charge. Telephone: 0870 442 2000. **Lord Leycester Hospital** – a beautiful group of timbered buildings dating from the late 14th century. Admission charge. Telephone: 01926 497797 for opening times.

11 The Shuckburgh Estate

The pastoral scene at Shuckburgh

Distance 5½ miles 🕓 3 hours
Terrain A hilly walk, with some level sections, over fields and some country lanes **Map:** OS Explorer 222 (GR 491628)

How to get there

From the A425 between Southam and Daventry turn off northwards by the church in Lower Shuckburgh, signed 'Grandborough'. **Parking:** In the lay-by just before the canal bridge.

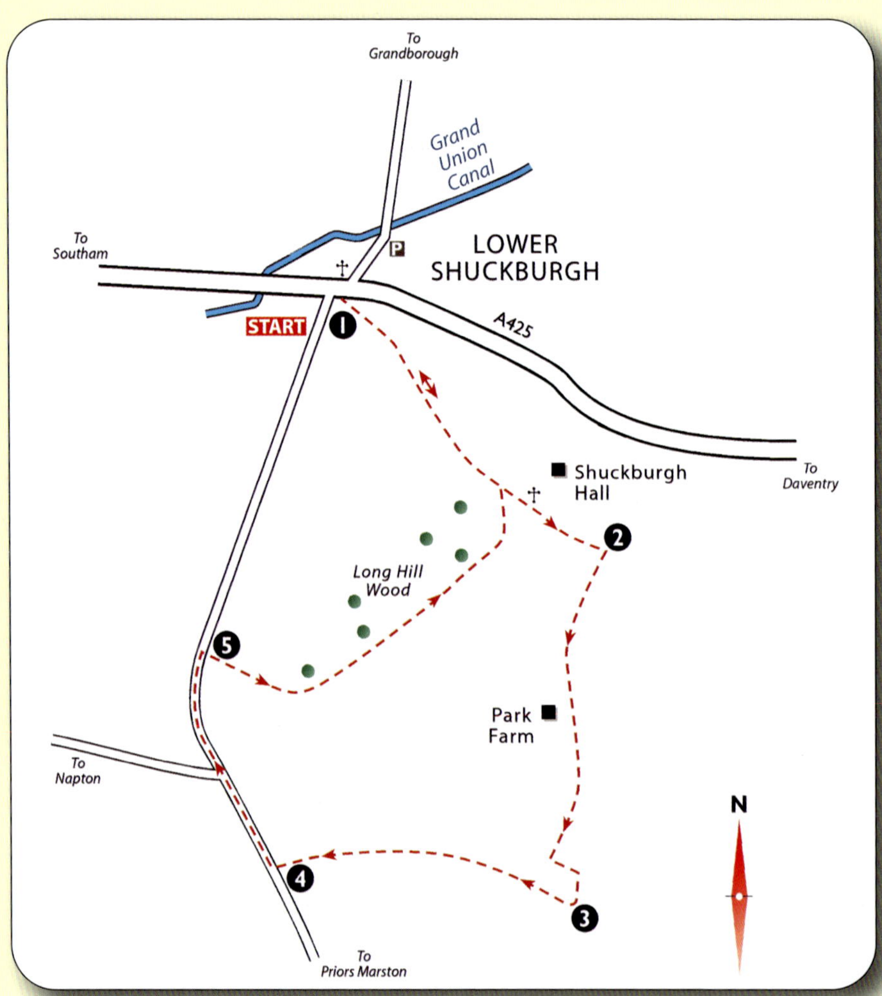

Introduction

This delightful walk goes through the Shuckburgh Estate and along the boundary of Warwickshire and Northamptonshire. The views are stunning, sometimes reaching as far as the Malvern Hills. It includes all the best elements of a good country walk: peace, views, varying landscapes and terrains and a feeling of elation at the beauty of it all. You may see deer on the estate, but you will meet very few people on your walk, it is a rural, off-the-beaten-track area. The route is waymarked throughout.

Refreshments

Just 2½ miles south of Lower Shuckburgh you will come to the **Holly Bush** pub in Holly Bush Lane, Priors Marston. An extensive menu is offered at this lovely old golden stone building set in the middle of a pretty Warwickshire village, including steak, pheasant, wild venison pie and Barbary duck breast. Food is served every day from 12 noon to 2 pm and 6.30 pm to 9.30 pm, except Monday lunchtime. Telephone: 01327 260934.

THE WALK

Walk back to the main road, passing the church and the village stocks.

You will pass Blackboy Cottages just to the left of the stocks. This used to be the village pub. However, there is a story that, many, many years ago, as the lord and lady of the manor were leaving the church one Sunday morning with all their children, someone sitting outside the pub made a suggestive remark about one of the daughters. That evening, the lord called his butler and told him to go to the pub at closing time and to fetch the front door key. The pub was locked up, never to open again!

Cross the main road and go through the gate to the left of the cottage. Bear diagonally left across the field, aiming for the right of the farm cottages on the hill. Go through a gate and immediately through another on the right. Turn left up a grassy slope to the right of the farm cottages. Continue on the same line and, 100 yards past the cottages, join the farm track down to a waymarked sign crossing a ditch. The path now sweeps left across a grassy field, up to the top of a hill. Look for a metal gate at the left edge of a hedge and pass through it.

Turn back to admire the magnificent views of Shuckburgh church and the Warwickshire countryside, stretching for miles.

Walk across the field, heading for the beacon, to pass through the gate by the beacon.

The beacon is one of a chain across England, originally used for warning of an invasion. Nowadays, they are lit for more peaceful and joyous occasions, such as the Queen's Golden Jubilee. The Malvern Hills can be seen from here on a good day.

Go straight ahead, through the next field, following the line of telegraph poles, to a wooden gate beside a metal gate. Walk ahead to the large

Lower Shuckburgh church

tree, passing under the telegraph wires, and keep straight ahead, aiming for the left of the farm buildings.

You will pass the estate church set upon a hill on the left. The church is a 'peculiar parish' meaning that it is not in a diocese, but is owned by the Shuckburgh family, who invite clergy to preach there. Shuckburgh Hall also comes into view on the left. The front was built in 1844, covering an older, timber-framed house. Neither the house nor the church is open to the public.

The path now joins a farm track coming in from the left. Walk along the gravelled track with the farm buildings on the right, to the gate by the lodge.

Turn right 30 yards after the gate. Walk along the estate track for just over ½ mile, through trees and past **Park Farm**. Keep straight ahead, with Park Farm and farmyard on the right, through a metal gate. Follow the track for 40 yards and, where the track ends, keep on the same line for about 220 yards, to a metal farm gate in the hedgerow straight ahead. Keep on the same line through the next field with the hedgerow on the left, to the next field boundary. Go through the metal gate in the corner and turn left. Keep the hedgerow on the left to the next field boundary. Go through the gate and turn right, keeping the hedgerow on the right. Walk to the far right corner of the field, pass through the metal gate and go over the stream to emerge on a farm track.

Turn right on the track and follow it for about ¾ mile, until it joins a road.

Turn right on the road and, after about 800 yards, turn right at the junction, signed to Lower Shuckburgh. Follow the road as it rises gently up the hill and passes through a metal gate.

Some 25 yards after the metal gate, turn right over a stile and walk straight ahead up a steep hill to the right corner of the field. Turn right over the double stile with a stream between, then left and on up the hill with **Long Hill Wood** on the left.

Turn left at the field corner where the wood ends and climb over a stile. On this section, the path is never more than about 40 yards from the edge of the wood. As you go ahead, set a course slightly to the right of the trees, to the brow of the rise. Keep left of the trig point on top of the hill. The path continues ahead, through a ridge and furrow field. Aim for the top left corner of the wood, and climb the stile to the right of a gate. Head now for the far right corner of the field, pass through the wide gap in the hedge at the side of the wood, and continue straight ahead for 30 yards. Take the path downhill, parallel to the wood, and head for a metal gate in the left corner of the field, about 250 yards away. Go through the gate and follow the path, keeping the woods on the left. The estate church comes into view once more. Cross the stile next to the wooden gate. Keep straight ahead for about 60 yards where the path bears left to rejoin the route you took on the outward journey.

Retrace your steps, past the beacon, using the village church as a guide. Cross the main road to return to the parking place.

PLACE OF INTEREST NEARBY

Braunston marina, located on the A45 a couple of miles north-west of Daventry, is at the heart of the waterways system. Two of the major canals meet here: the Oxford Canal and the Grand Union Canal.

12 Aston Cantlow

The Cider Mill at Walcote

Distance 4½ miles 2½ hours
Terrain Mostly level, with a few gentle gradients; field paths, some country lanes and 300 yards of main road **Map:** OS Explorer 205 (GR 138598)

How to get there

Take the B4089 between Alcester and Wootton Wawen. Turn off in the village of Little Alne, signed 'Aston Cantlow'. After about ¼ mile turn right and follow the road into the village. **Parking:** In the main street, near the King's Head.

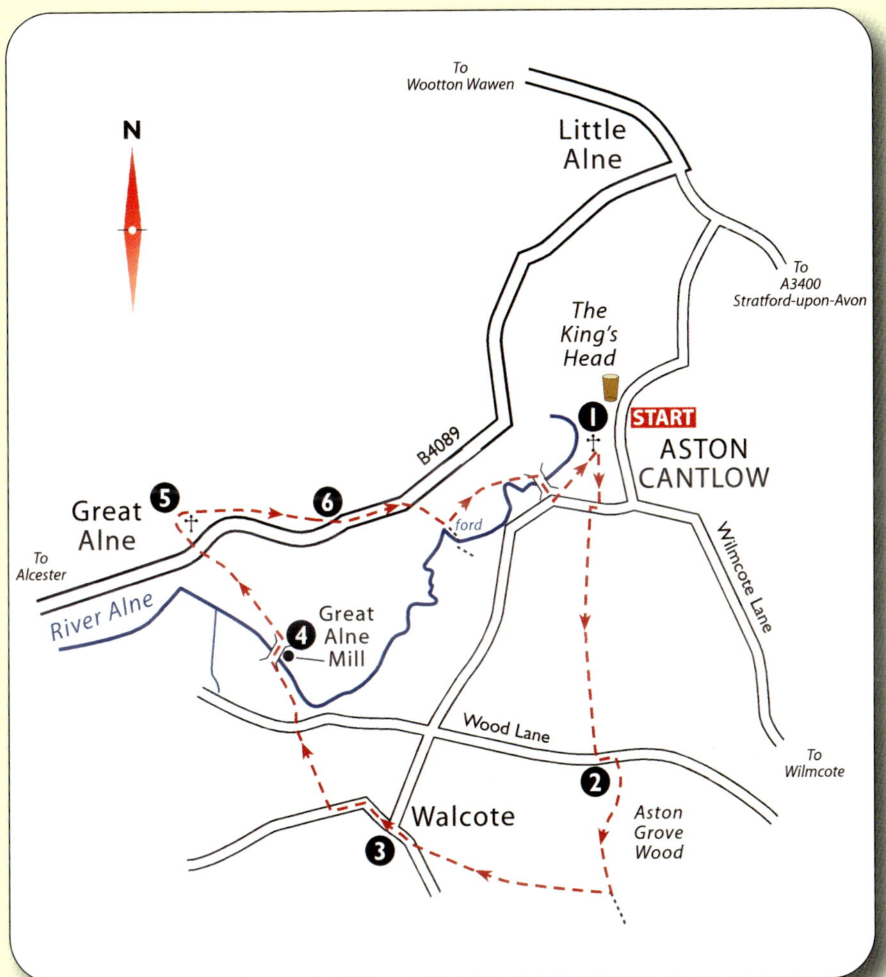

Introduction

This pretty walk starts in the village of Aston Cantlow, named after a local family, de Cantilupe. Shakespeare's parents are said to have been married in the church here and the guildhall in the village dates from the 16th century. The first half of the walk follows the Arden Way, and the path also passes through a Site of Special Scientific Interest. Walcote is a peaceful hamlet with pretty houses, including the Cider Mill, with a huge, old, original cider press in the front garden.

Refreshments

The 15th-century **King's Head** in Aston Cantlow has low beams, flagged stone floors and open fireplaces. Legend has it that Shakespeare's parents held their wedding reception here. Friendly staff serve excellent sandwiches and an interesting menu, including duck, for which the King's Head has a long-established reputation. Food is available from 12 noon to 2.30 pm and 6.30 pm to 9.30 pm on Monday to Friday, 12 noon to 2.30 pm and 6.30 pm to 9.30 pm on Saturday and 12.30 pm to 3 pm on Sunday; the pub closes in the early evening on Sunday. Telephone: 01789 488242.

THE WALK

Take the road to the left of the **King's Head**, to the church. Enter the churchyard through the lychgate and take the left footpath. At the far side of the churchyard, walk along the footpath and over the footbridge. Follow the path, which goes off at about '10 o'clock' to the far boundary. Cross the stile and the road and follow the wide farm track opposite, with a hedge on the right. The walk now joins the **Arden Way** for the next 2 miles.

The Arden Way is a 26-mile offshoot of the Heart of England Way, starting and finishing at Henley-in-Arden. Rural in character, it traces old paths and routes through the ancient Forest of Arden.

Go through the gap at the end of the field and, after about 130 yards, where the track veers off to the right, keep straight ahead, through the next field, with the hedge on the right. Cross the stile in the far right corner into **Wood Lane**.

Turn left for about 80 yards and then right through a wooden gate. Follow the wide track up the slope to the edge of a wood.

This is Aston Grove and Withycombe Wood, a Site of Special Scientific Interest. The woods are amongst the finest in Warwickshire.

Follow the path along the edge of the trees and enter the wood through a gate. Continue for about 250 yards to a path junction. Turn right to leave the woods through a metal kissing gate and enter the field. Keep the hedge on the right as the path goes down a gentle slope. Keep straight ahead all the way to the field boundary. Turn right through a gap in the hedge, and then immediately left. Keep straight ahead, with the hedge on the left. The walk now passes through three fields and emerges through a metal kissing gate onto a track.

Turn right to join the road and keep straight ahead.

This is the pretty village of Walcote, where almost every house is asking to be photographed.

The road bends to the left at a letterbox.

Just by the letterbox is Cider Mill Cottage, with an original cider press in its front garden. Cider was produced here through the 19th century and up to 1947.

The church at point 5 of the walk

Follow the road round and, in 175 yards, turn right over a wooden stile, just by the old vicarage. Here the route leaves the **Arden Way**. Walk through the field, with the hedge on the right, and cross a wooden stile. At the end of the next field there is a double stile and footbridge. Walk straight ahead to a metal kissing gate, which leads onto a road. Turn left and immediately right over a footbridge into a grassy field. The path goes straight across the field and then sweeps to the left. Pass to the left of the mill buildings and look for a bridge across the **River Alne**. Cross the bridge and turn right. Walk across the gravel drive and turn left into the lane.

After 50 yards, turn left to walk across the wide grass verge and over a stile. Cross the field right at about '1 o'clock' to a wooden kissing gate in the hedge. Maintain the same line to cross the next field to a gap in the hedge. Cross the dismantled railway to a metal gate and make for the top left corner of the field. Go over the stile and keep straight ahead to the right of a brick building, to go through a wooden gate and onto a road. Turn right onto the road and then left through a wooden gate signed to the church.

Follow the path, through the churchyard, and turn left down a footpath opposite the church front door. Go through the kissing gate at the bottom and turn right along the field. In 60 yards turn right over a stile and diagonally left across a field to a wooden kissing gate. Walk along a path between hedges and then buildings, to join the road. Cross over the road and take the footpath slightly to the right on the opposite side of the road. Follow the footpath, alongside a fence at first, then through a pretty copse. Keep straight ahead at the path junction, eventually emerging from the trees beside a cricket field. The path joins a drive. Turn right and at the main road turn left.

Walk along the road for 350 yards and, where the road bends to the left, turn right down a rough track. About 25 yards after passing an electricity substation, look very carefully for a path on the left hidden amongst the trees. Follow the path down through the trees, past an old railway bridge and over the stile at the bottom. Turn half left and aim for a stile in the left hedge, about 80 yards from the left corner of the long field. Cross the stile, the footbridge and a second stile, and follow the path as it meanders along the river bank. It eventually arrives at a footbridge. Cross the footbridge and enter a caravan park. Walk across the grass and then turn left onto a gravel drive. Follow the drive round to the right, over a bridge and onto the road. Turn left and almost immediately left again, through a wooden gate and along a footpath, which leads back to the church.

PLACE OF INTEREST NEARBY

Mary Arden's House in Wilmcote, approximately 3½ miles to the south-east of Aston Cantlow, was the home of Shakespeare's grandparents, and of his mother, Mary Arden. Here you can see and experience how life was lived in Shakespeare's times. There is a nature trail and rare breeds of cattle, sheep and pigs. Open throughout the year. Telephone for details of opening times: 01789 201806.

13 Hampton Lucy

On the way to Hampton Lucy church

Distance 4½ miles 2½ hours
Terrain Gently undulating **Map:** OS Explorer 205 (GR 255570)

How to get there

Hampton Lucy lies south-west of Warwick. At junction 15 of the M40, take the A429 towards Stow. After 3 miles turn right for Charlecote, and in less than a mile take the right turn signed to Hampton Lucy. Cross the river bridge and after 100 yards turn left on the road towards Stratford-upon-Avon. **Parking:** Off road parking is available 200 yards after the Boar's Head pub, by the children's play area.

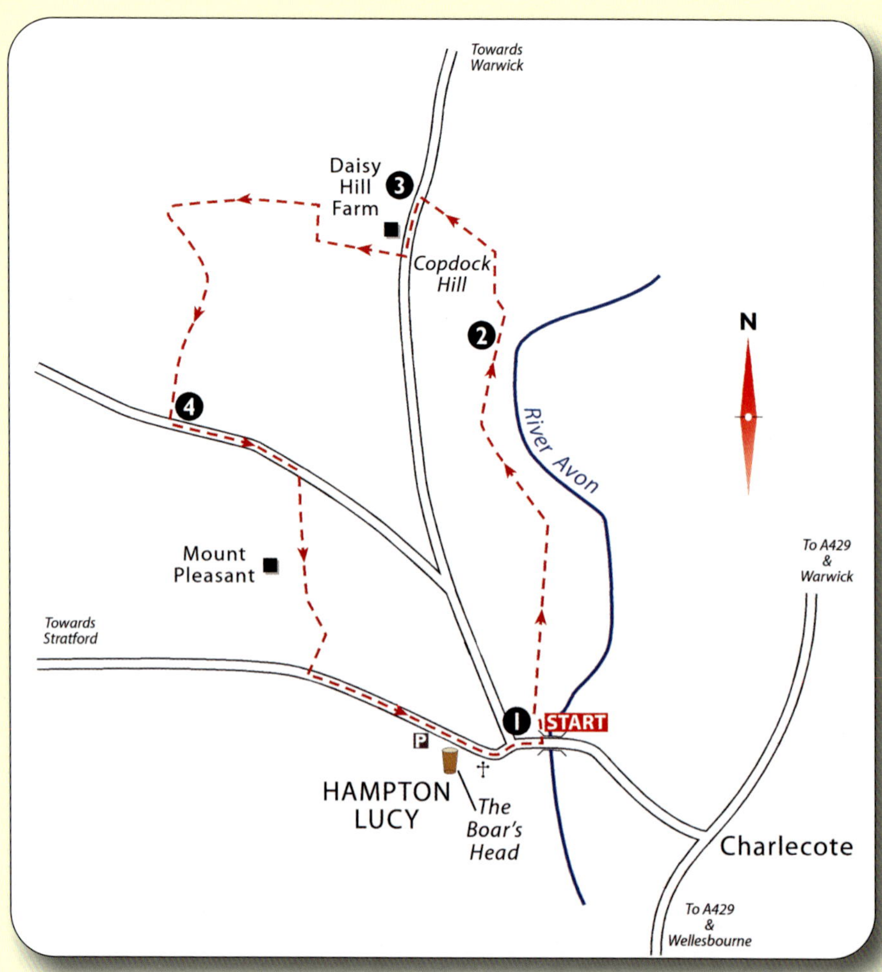

Introduction

Hampton Lucy would have been well known to Shakespeare. The village church, St Peter's, is most impressive for such a small community; it was built by one of the owners of the nearby Charlecote Park. There are excellent views from many points, towards both Stratford-upon-Avon and Warwick. The River Avon runs in the valley alongside the route of the walk at the beginning. The circuit is mostly on field paths, with a couple of short stretches of country lanes. Step back in time, away from noisy roads and the hurly-burly of busy every day life and relish the peace and quiet.

Refreshments

The **Boar's Head** is situated in the centre of Hampton Lucy. It dates back to the 17th century when it was a cider house. The present kitchen was once a mortuary. There is a sheltered rear garden for sunny days and the interior is attractive and cosy, with a log fire in the winter. Food is served Monday to Thursday at lunchtime and in the evening, and all day on Friday, Saturday and Sunday. Telephone: 01789 840533.

The **Orangery** at Charlecote Park (see 'Place of Interest Nearby') serves morning coffee and afternoon tea with sandwiches and pastries and also lunches. Telephone for opening hours: 01789 470277.

THE WALK

Walk back to the white bridge over the **River Avon**. Turn left immediately before the bridge, along a tarmac path by the river.

On the opposite bank is Charlecote Mill, a working watermill. Corn is still ground here, and there are occasional open days. Ring for further details: 01789 842072.

After 80 yards, turn left before a five-bar gate, walk along the gently rising path as it follows the field boundary and then pass through a gate.

Through the trees, there are glimpses of the River Avon meandering along the valley below and the distant countryside beyond.

Continue along the path as it goes through a green corridor of grasses, bushes and trees. Soon you will pass a bench and go through another gate. Continue along the ridge and, after 180 yards, at the path junction, take the higher path to the left (ignore the bridlepath on the right). Along here there are good views on the left towards **Stratford-upon-Avon** and the obelisk on the **Welcombe Hills**.

The obelisk is 120 ft high and was erected in 1896 to the memory of the Phillips family, who were politicians and manufacturers of cotton.

Continue along the path, keeping the hedge on the right.

The path now rises gently and enters a wide space at the corner of two fields, veering away from the hedge and passing to the left of a line of oak trees. Follow the path to the top of **Copdock Hill**, keeping the woods on the right. When the top of the hill is reached, the path turns left and offers a 180° view, with

Warwick at the centre marked by the soaring tower of **St Mary's church**.

St Mary's church in Warwick is a landmark for miles around. Its tower is 174 ft high and was rebuilt in the 17th century after the first tower proved unstable.

After 230 yards, look carefully for a narrow grassy unsigned path descending between old fence posts to the right. This soon meets a country lane.

Turn left onto the lane, and, after 100 yards, turn right up the drive to **Daisy Hill Farm**. Follow the drive until approximately 100 yards before the farm buildings and turn left through the gate, across a small field and through another gate. Continue straight ahead, aiming for the left end of a hedgerow. Go through the gate and turn left down the hill, keeping the hedgerow on the left. Cross the stile at the bottom and go straight ahead up the hill, keeping the hedgerow on the left and, at the path junction, take the left path, following the perimeter of the field. Continue to the field corner where the path passes through a wooded glade. Continue straight ahead until the path meets a road.

Turn left along the road and, after 500 yards, turn right along a gravelled drive to **Mount Pleasant**. Near the house, the drive sweeps to the right, but the path goes straight ahead, to the left of the buildings, across a grassy area. Keep straight ahead and pass a stile in the far left corner of the field. Follow the perimeter of the field with the hedge on the left for about 200 yards and then turn left over a stile immediately after a telegraph pole. Turn right and keep the hedge on the right, all the way to the country lane and turn left, back to **Hampton Lucy**

PLACE OF INTEREST NEARBY

The National Trust's **Charlecote Park** is well worth a visit. The house has an Elizabethan appearance, but is mainly 19th-century. The kitchens are set out as if for use, and the brewery, which made the beer for the estate, can be visited. Deer roam in the extensive grounds. Telephone for details of opening times: 01789 470277.

14 Stratford-upon-Avon

The Falcon Hotel in Chapel Street

Distance 2½ miles At least 2 hours
Terrain Level; town footpaths and grass **Map:** OS Explorer 205 (GR 205550)

How to get there

Enter Stratford-upon-Avon on the A439 from Warwick. **Parking:** Where the road becomes one way, keep to the right lane and, in about 100 yards, turn into Bridgefoot multi-storey ('pay on foot') car park.

Introduction

William Shakespeare is Stratford's most famous son, and the town is visited by people from all over the world, keen to walk in the Bard's footsteps.

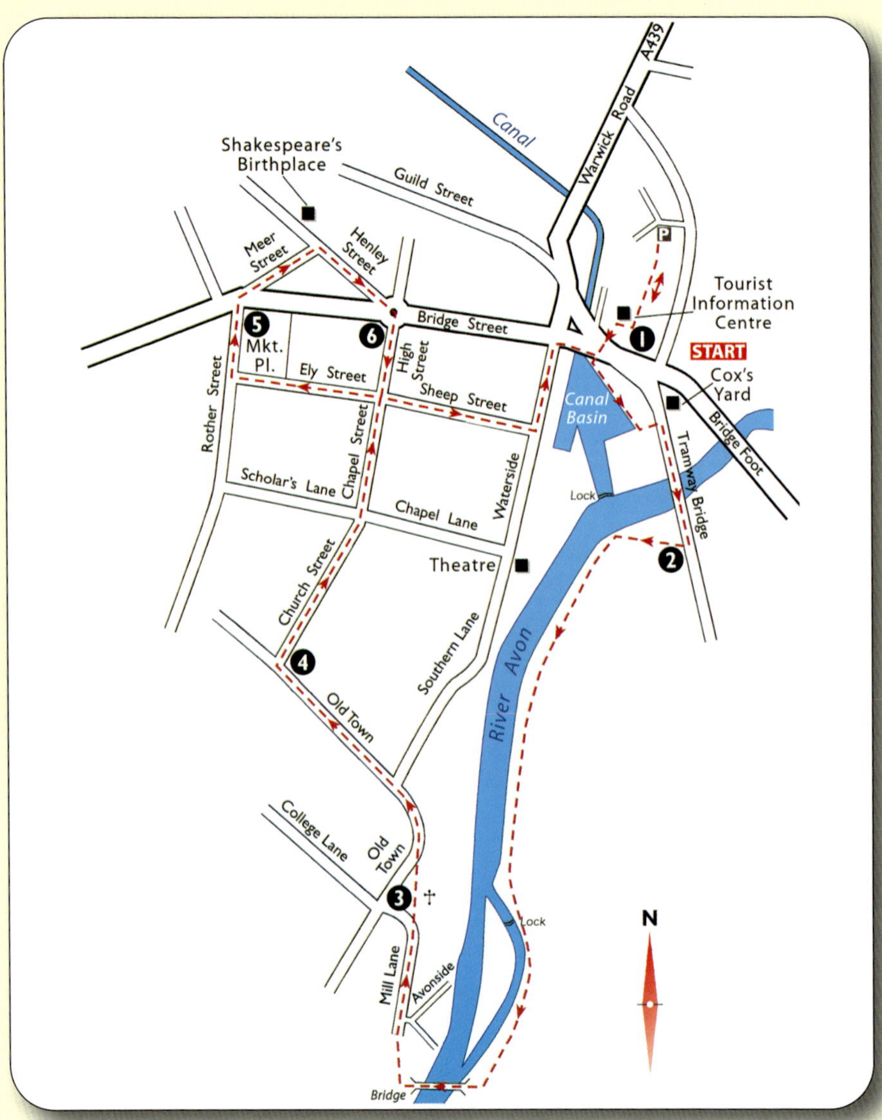

The house where he was born and raised, the school that he attended and the house where he lived in later days can all be visited. But the town has far more to offer and this walk will take you past many delightful buildings, along the river and by the theatre. There is so much to see along the way that, although this is the shortest walk in the book, you should allow plenty of time to complete it.

Refreshments

The choice is so great that it is almost unnecessary to mention one particular place. However, **Cox's Yard**, right by the Avon at Clopton Bridge, is in a lovely position and serves a wide variety of food all day long. Here you can have a coffee, a lunchtime snack, afternoon tea or an evening meal. Telephone: 01789 404600.

THE WALK

Leave the car park by the pedestrian entrance and walk straight ahead to the **Tourist Information Centre**. Cross the road immediately in front of the TIC, turn right and in a few yards turn left, down the steps, to walk along the **Stratford Canal Basin**. Follow the perimeter of the basin, passing the **Gower Memorial** on the left. Ahead on the right there is a lock, which allows boats from the canal to join the **River Avon**. Turn left alongside the lock to **Cox's Yard** and then turn right to cross the river on the **Tramway Bridge**.

The Stratford & Moreton Tramway opened in 1826 to carry coal brought from the Black Country via the Stratford Canal, and to take the fruits of the Vale of Evesham on the return journey. It used horse drawn trams, but it was never successful and was eventually dismantled.

The Stratford Canal fell into disrepair over the years and was due to be closed in 1955, but fortunately public protest and the National Trust saved the day. The gaily-painted narrowboats moored in the basin add a picturesque touch to the waterside scene.

Turn right at the end of the bridge and join the path along the river.

There are excellent views of the Royal Shakespeare Theatre on the opposite bank.

Walk along the path as it follows the course of the **Avon** to the weir and the **Colin P. Witter Lock**. The path skirts the lock and continues straight ahead, still with the river on the right. Ahead there is a footbridge, which crosses the river. Take this and, at the far end, turn right immediately, along a tarmac path, passing **Lucy's Mill** and **Avonside**. The path joins **Mill Lane** and, where the lane bends to the left, go straight ahead into **Holy Trinity churchyard**.

Shakespeare's birthplace

③

After 50 yards the path turns right to reach the main door of the church.

Shakespeare is buried in Holy Trinity church.

Turn left on the flagged path, through the avenue of lime trees, to leave the churchyard by the wrought-iron gates and enter **Old Town**. Follow the road straight ahead, passing **Southern Lane**.

Just after passing Southern Lane, you will reach Hall's Croft, which was owned by John Hall, a Stratford physician who married Shakespeare's daughter Susannah.

This attractive Tudor building dates from the early 16th century.

Keep on the same path and turn right at the next junction into **Church Street**.

As you walk along Church Street, you will pass a row of timber-framed almhouses built in the 15th century. Next door is King Edward VI Grammar School for Boys, attended by Shakespeare and still in use.

Continue along **Church Street**, going straight ahead at the next junction into **Chapel Street**.

Take time to look at New Place, on the right as you enter Chapel Street. New Place was Shakespeare's final home in Stratford. Sadly the house was later demolished by an eccentric owner who grew tired of sightseers, and only the cellars and foundations are visible. It must have been a splendid house in its day. However, the gardens are a delight, free to enter and well worth a visit. The entrance is in Chapel Lane.

Turn left at the next junction, into **Ely Street** and walk to the end of the street and then right into the **Market Place**.

Take a look at the American Fountain near the middle of the Market Square. An American journalist, George W. Childs, presented it to the town in 1887.

Turn right in front of the fountain, walk to the crossing and cross the road. Pass around the **National Westminster Bank** and turn right into **Meer Street**, behind the bank. At the end of Meer Street turn left into **Henley Street** for a few yards, to see **Shakespeare's Birthplace**.

Shakespeare was born here on 23rd April 1564. His father was a glove maker, amongst other things, and part of the house was his shop and workroom.

Turn round and retrace your steps past the top of **Meer Street** and along **Henley Street** to the roundabout. Here take the second right into **High Street**.

Walk along **High Street** to the first junction and turn left down **Sheep Street**. Continue to the end of **Sheep Street** into **Waterside** and look to the right to see the **Royal Shakespeare Memorial Theatre**. Turn left along **Waterside** to return to the start of the walk.

PLACES OF INTEREST NEARBY

Shakespeare's Birthplace in Henley Street (see point 5). Telephone: 01789 201813. The **Royal Shakespeare Theatre**, where plays are performed throughout the year (see point 6). For tickets telephone: 0844 800 1110; for details of tours of the theatre: 0844 800 1114. **Sightseeing trips on the Avon** are available throughout the year. Contact Bancroft Cruisers: 01789 269669.

15 Welford-on-Avon

Some of the charming cottages in Welford

Distance 4 miles 2½ hours
Terrain Mainly level, with a few gentle slopes, over field paths and a short distance on roads **Map:** OS Explorer 205 (GR 150518)

How to get there

Taking the B439 between Stratford-upon-Avon and Bidford-on-Avon, turn off southwards to Welford-on-Avon about 4 miles from Stratford. **Parking:** In Chapel Street, not far from the village maypole.

Introduction

Welford-on-Avon has the honour of possessing the tallest maypole in England. In fact it was the tallest in the world until a part of it broke off! The

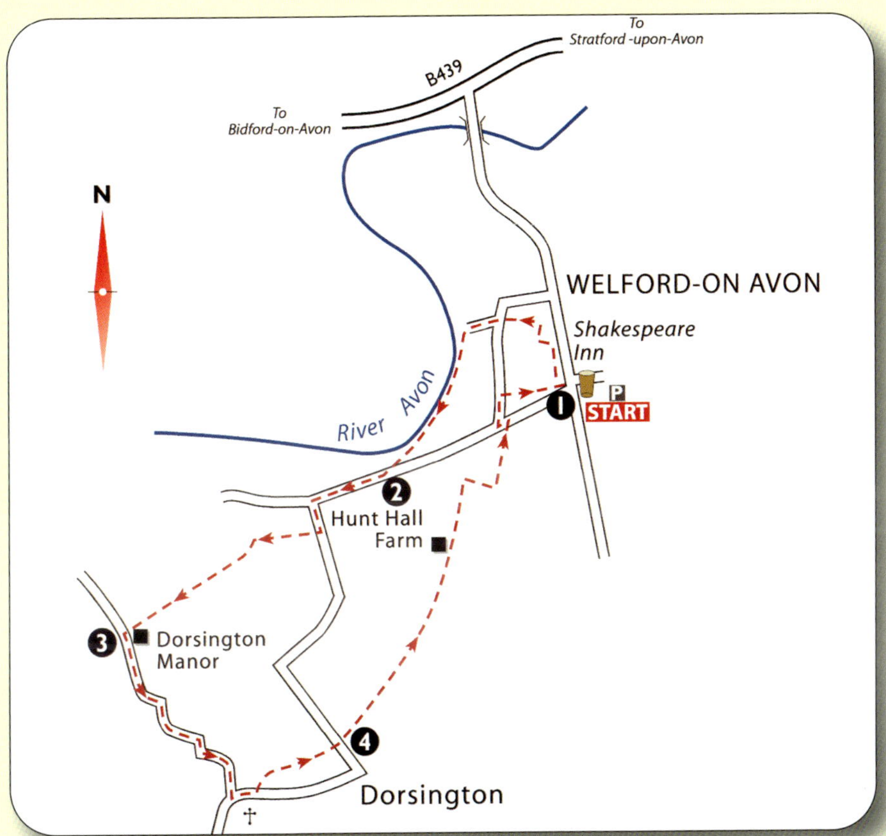

village schoolchildren dance around it each June. Ten Penny Cottage located in Boat Lane is a real 'chocolate box cottage' – its picture was used at one time by Cadbury's for the lid of its chocolate boxes. The walk goes along the banks of the River Avon, following the Avon Valley Way, and then continues through the rolling south Warwickshire countryside, with far-reaching views of the river valley and the Cotswolds.

Refreshments

The **Shakespeare Inn** in Chapel Street prides itself on serving fresh, locally sourced food wherever possible, and the menu includes Welford sausages, steak and ale pie, steak and sea bass. You can eat here from 12 noon to 2.30 pm and 6.30 pm to 9.30 pm on Tuesday to Sunday and 5.30 pm to 9.30 pm on Monday. Telephone: 01789 750443.

THE WALK

Walk back to the maypole and cross **High Street** to go through a metal kissing gate and along the footpath. In 100 yards turn right. Follow the path, keeping straight ahead at a footpath junction. Now the path winds along the bottom of gardens, emerging at a road. Go straight across into **Mill Lane**. Turn left at the end of the lane, signed '**Avon Valley Way**'. Follow the path through a caravan site and onto a footpath, with a fence on the right.

The footpath runs along the bank above the River Avon. It is possible to get closer to the river on a narrower path used by anglers, but do return to the main path in order to follow the route.

Keep straight ahead for about 600 yards, with a wire field fence on the left, to arrive at a path junction. Take the left path and go up the first flight of steps. Turn sharp right at the wooden bench, continuing up a grassy path for 150 yards and through a gate to emerge onto a road.

Turn right on the road for 400 yards, and then turn left at the junction, signed 'Dorsington 1¼ miles'.

There are beautiful views over the Avon Valley on the right.

After 150 yards, turn right, over a stile.

There are magnificent views of the Cotswolds from here.

Keep the field boundary close to the right and walk through an avenue of small trees to go through a wooden gate on the right, just before a telegraph pole. Turn left, following the line of telegraph wires for 150 yards, to another wooden gate in the field hedge. Go through the gate, cross the lane and continue through another wooden gate to follow a wide footpath around the boundary of a field. Go through the wooden gate at the left corner of the field and turn right, following a line of telegraph wires.

Pass through two fields. Towards the end of the second field the path bends to the left, through a metal farm gate, over a concrete bridge and along a track to the road. **Dorsington Manor** is on the left.

Turn left on the road for about ½ mile, to **Dorsington** (the Heart of England Way now joins the walk as far as the village). At the junction turn left, signed 'Welford-on-Avon 2½ miles. In 170 yards, just beyond **Church Farm**, turn left through a gate and bear diagonally right across a field to a wooden gate. Go through the gate to a footbridge in the left corner of the next field. Walk straight across the next field, maintaining the same line, aiming for the stile on the far side of the field.

Cross the stile and the road and go through a metal kissing gate. Pass to the right of a clump of trees and head diagonally for the left corner of the field. Go through the metal kissing gate, over a wooden footbridge and turn right, keeping the hedge on the right, to the next stile. Keep straight ahead to go through a metal gate. Here the path veers slightly to the left. Aim for the right of the farm buildings ahead.

Pass through the metal gate by the farm buildings, keep straight ahead for about 40 yards and then go right and left through the farmyard, onto a tarmac lane. In about 300 yards look for a narrow gap in the hedge on the right. Cross the footbridge and go through the metal kissing gate. Turn left and then right, following the perimeter of the field. At the field corner turn left through a metal gate. Go straight across the field to a metal kissing gate onto a grassy track through a wooded area. The footpath emerges onto a road. Cross the road into **Headland Road**. After 120 yards, turn right through a wooden gate onto a footpath. Follow the footpath between the hedges straight ahead, neither turning right nor left, to reach **High Street** and the parking place.

Welford's maypole is the tallest in the country

PLACE OF INTEREST NEARBY

The splendid **Ragley Hall**, which is 2 miles south-west of Alcester, is a Palladian house set in grounds designed by Lancelot 'Capability' Brown. A rose garden, a woodland walk and an adventure playground for children are among the attractions. Telephone: 0800 093 0290.

Drive and Stroll

16 Combrook and Compton Verney

The view across to Compton Verney

Distance 3½ miles 🕓 1½ hours
Terrain Some gentle slopes, field paths, country lanes and a little road walking **Map:** OS Explorer 206 (GR 308517)

How to get there

Take the B4086 between Wellesbourne and the B4100 at Warmington. A little less than a mile east of the Fosse Way (the B4455), turn off southwards, signed to Combrook. Continue along the road to the village and turn right by the church. **Parking:** You can leave your car in the no through road by the church.

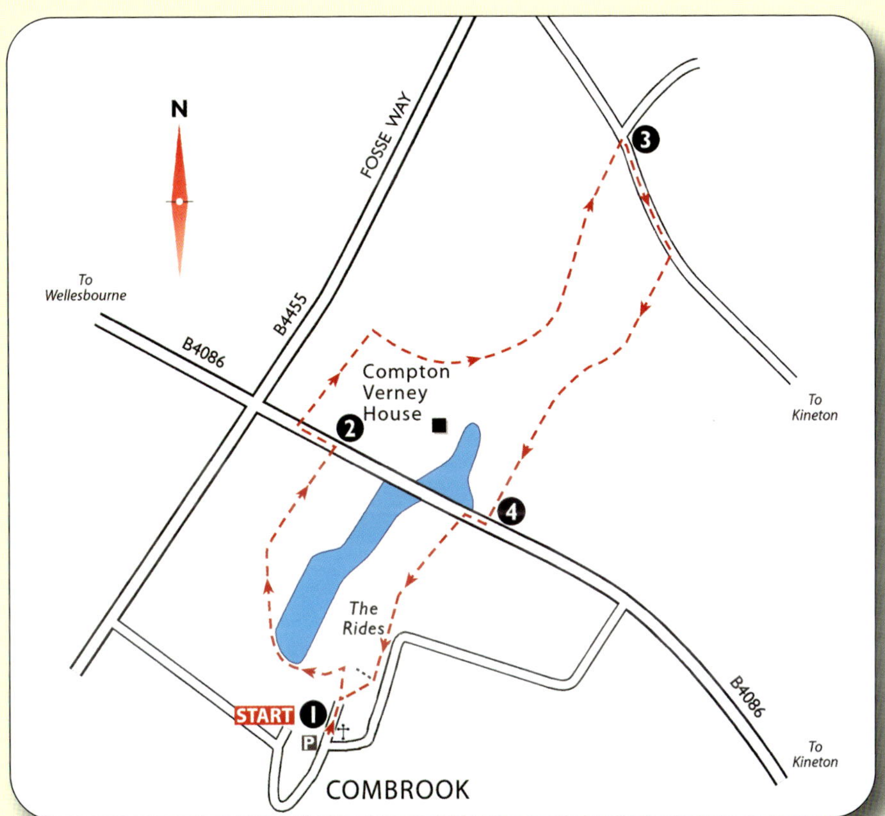

Introduction

The walk begins and ends in the pretty village of Combrook, just off the Fosse Way, and passes through the landscaped grounds of Compton Verney, a restored stately home, now an art gallery. A pleasant section leads into a wood called The Rides, which is deep and green and peaceful. Linking all of these are long expanses of rolling arable farmland, bridleways and footpaths, offering views over the heart of Warwickshire.

Refreshments

On the B4086 at Wellesbourne, approximately 3 miles from Combrook, the **King's Head** dates back to the 1600s, when it was a coaching inn. It was subsequently used as a hospital for wounded soldiers from the Battle of Edgehill. Three centuries later it offered respite to the pilots at the nearby

Wellesbourne aerodrome during the Second World War. A wide choice of good pub food is served every day: 12 noon to 10 pm on Monday to Saturday and 12 noon to 9.30 pm on Sunday (except 24th, 25th and 31st December and 1st January). Telephone: 0845 11 26 075.

THE WALK

Combrook, sometimes spelt Combroke, is a small village that housed the workers of the nearby Compton Verney estate. The village is one of the best examples of an estate village in the country.

Walk on along the lane where you parked, past a well on the right, and turn left onto a footpath immediately before some thatched cottages. The footpath rises gently and turns right along a grassy track. Keep straight ahead, with the lake on the right and follow the path as it swings right and enters the woods alongside the lake. Passing through the wooden gate at the end of the wood, the path veers slightly left away from the lake to a waymarker. Here the path goes slightly right, up a little incline to another waymarker in the field to the right of two houses. Walk on to the far corner of the field, through a metal gate and along a tarmacked farm track to join the main road.

Turn left and walk uphill for 200 yards, then turn right onto a tarmacked drive beside **Compton Verney Lodge**. Continue straight ahead and follow the drive as it turns right in front of a bungalow. Go straight ahead through the metal gate and onto a grassy bridleway. Follow the track as it bends left. On the right, **Compton Verney House** and the **Adam Bridge** can be seen.

Compton Verney House was rebuilt in the early 18th century and extended by Robert Adam later in the same century. The grounds were landscaped by Lancelot 'Capability' Brown. The house was bought in a dilapidated state by Sir Peter Moores, of Littlewoods Pools, and has now been restored as an art gallery, restaurant and venue for corporate activities.

Follow this bridleway all the way to the road, about ¾ mile away.

Turn right on the road and follow it to the bottom of the slope and up the other side to a footpath on the right. Go through the wooden gate onto a wide grassy track for a little less than ½ mile. Pass through a kissing gate and walk

Compton Verney is set in landscaped gardens

straight ahead across the field, heading for the woods on the opposite field boundary. You will see a waymarker by **Compton Verney** car park.

Pass through the kissing gate across the car park. Turn left on the road to join the main road. Turn right and, at the bus stop about 30 yards along the road, turn left onto the footpath. Set a course of about 45° right, following the waymarker to the top of the field. Look for a waymarker pointing into the woods. Walk straight through the woods, past the stile and, ignoring the path to the right, head diagonally downhill to the right of a row of houses. Turn left to return to the church.

PLACE OF INTEREST NEARBY

The Grade I listed **Compton Verney** is set in a delightful position, amidst huge man-made lakes and landscaped grounds. It houses an art gallery and there is also a café. Telephone: 01926 645500.

17 Radway, Ratley and Edgehill

The view from Edgehill

Distance 3¾ miles 2½ hours
Terrain Mostly footpaths, some farm tracks and short sections of road; some steep ascents and descents **Map:** OS Explorer 206 (GR 369478)

How to get there

Take the B4086 between Wellesbourne and the B4100 at Warmington. About 3 miles south-east of Kineton, turn off southwards, signed to Radway. Continue through the village towards the church and then turn left into West End. **Parking:** There is on-street parking in West End.

Introduction

Warwickshire is a gently undulating county in the main, so this walk, with its steep hill climbs and descents, offers a very different experience. It passes through three pretty villages, where many of the houses are built of the warm

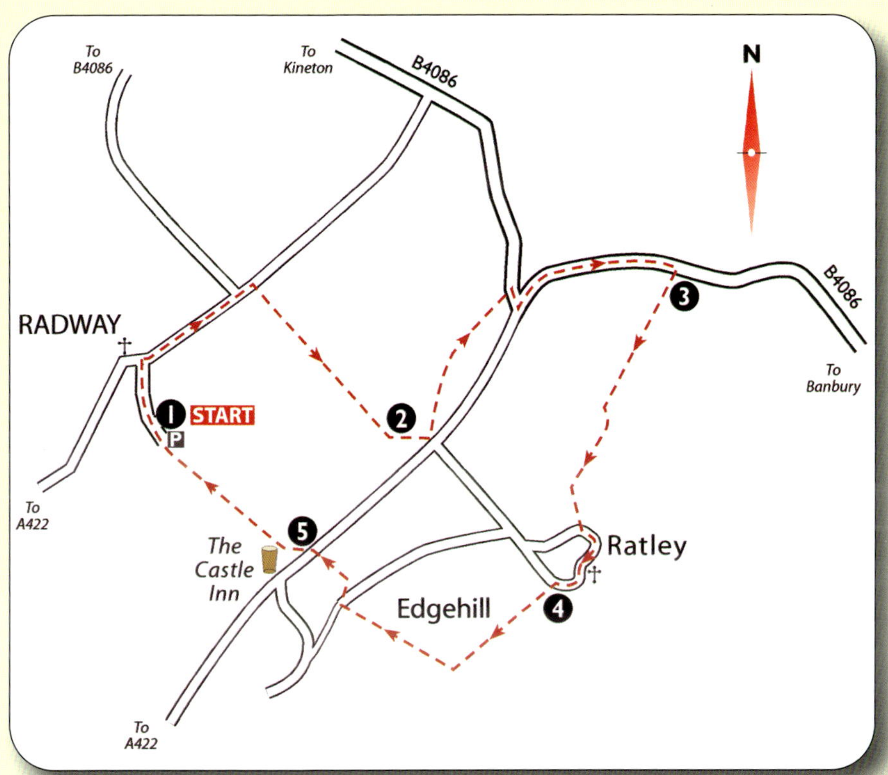

local ironstone. Ratley is the highest village in the county, Edgehill has the Castle public house, originally an 18th-century folly, and Radway lies at the foot of the hill, close to the battlefield. It was on this flat plain that the first battle of the English Civil War was fought, on Sunday, 23rd October 1642. This circuit has much to offer: wonderful walking country, charming villages and a wealth of history.

Refreshments

The walk passes close to the fascinating **Castle Inn** in Edgehill. Inside this unusual castellated building there are many pictures and artefacts of the Civil War battle. An excellent range of good home-cooked food is offered, including fish, rice and pasta dishes. The bars are open all day, every day. Food is served from 12 noon to 9 pm daily (sandwiches and ploughman's only between 2 pm and 5 pm). Telephone: 01295 670255.

THE WALK

Walk back to the junction and turn right, to go past **Radway Grange** and some pretty thatched cottages. Beyond the bus shelter, turn right up **Norton's Lane**. Follow the path as it passes a cottage garden to a wooden kissing gate. In about 30 yards, go through another kissing gate and walk straight ahead, up the field, to the woods ahead, keeping the wire fence on the left.

After this steep climb, sit on the stone seat to admire the fantastic view, and imagine the scene as the Royalists and Parliamentarians faced each other on the plain below. One in ten soldiers was killed in the battle, some of whom are buried in a mass grave behind Ratley church. The result was indecisive, with both sides claiming victory.

Enter the woods and turn left then immediately right on a steep path through the woods. Climb a long flight of steps, known as **Jacob's Ladder**, and, after another flight of stone steps, turn left just before the path reaches the road. Continue through the woods for about 600 yards, ignoring paths going off to the left. The path emerges onto the road at a T-junction. Cross the road and walk straight ahead to follow the road signed 'Banbury B4086', using the footpath along the left-hand side. The road passes some houses on the left. Some 80 yards after the last house, look for a gap in the hedge on the right side of the road, under the telegraph wires, waymarked '**Centenary Way**'.

The walk now follows a section of the Warwickshire Centenary Way, a recreational footpath, established in 1989 to celebrate the 100th anniversary of Warwickshire County Council. It runs north/south through the county.

Follow the path straight ahead downhill across the field to the field boundary ahead. Cross over the footbridge into the next field. The path ahead rises gently, to meet a kissing gate in the top left corner of the field. The path now passes between a hedgerow on the left and a wire fence on the right. After about 100 yards, just past the end of the wire fence, turn right onto a path at right angles to the hedge, straight across the field. Go through a kissing gate and, in 20 yards, turn left over a stone stile. Follow the path downhill to the very bottom right corner, climb the stile and walk straight ahead to join the road in **Ratley**. Turn left, down to the village green, and then right at the junction.

The Rose and Crown pub is on the left, if you are in need of midway refreshment. As you pass the church, take a moment to look in the churchyard and see the old preaching cross, dating from around the same time as the church itself. Soldiers who died in the Battle of Edgehill are buried in mounds behind the church.

Walk past the church and in a short distance, where the road bends right, turn left towards a farm. Walk along here for 50 yards and then turn right immediately before **Manor Farm**, through a gap in the hedge and over a stile. Walk up the little rise, setting a course slightly to the right. Pass under the telegraph wires and aim for a stile on the right side of the field at the bottom of the slope.

Cross the stile and go straight up the field to the opposite corner and over the wooden stile. Turn right onto the farm track, which eventually joins the road. Turn right on the road and then, after 60 yards, turn left down a narrow footpath to emerge onto another road in **Edgehill**.

The Castle Inn is a short distance along the road to the left. The tower was built by Sanderson Miller in the style of Guy's Tower at Warwick Castle.

Turn left and in a few yards turn right by a telegraph pole, down a flight of stone steps. Follow the path as it goes downhill, with a good handrail alongside. At the footpath crossroads go straight ahead through a wooden kissing gate and into the field.

Walk down the hill to the kissing gate in the right corner of the field. Keep the fence on the left in the next field and walk to the far left corner. Go through the kissing gate, keep straight ahead on the farm track and back into **West End**.

PLACE OF INTEREST NEARBY

Upton House, a National Trust property, is to the south of Radway, just off the A422. A 17th-century mansion set in fine terraced gardens, it houses one of the Trust's most important art collections and has an impressive display of Sèvres porcelain. Telephone: 01295 670266.

18 Tysoe

Delightful cottages in Tysoe

Distance 3¾ miles 2 hours
Terrain Two steep gradients, some field paths and about a mile of country road **Map:** OS Explorer 206 (GR 334435)

How to get there

Take the A422 between Stratford-upon-Avon and Banbury and turn off southwards to Tysoe about 10 miles from Stratford. Drive all the way through the villages of Lower Tysoe and Middle Tysoe, and at the far end of Upper Tysoe, follow the sign to Shipston. **Parking:** In a lay-by about 30 yards past the speed de-restriction sign.

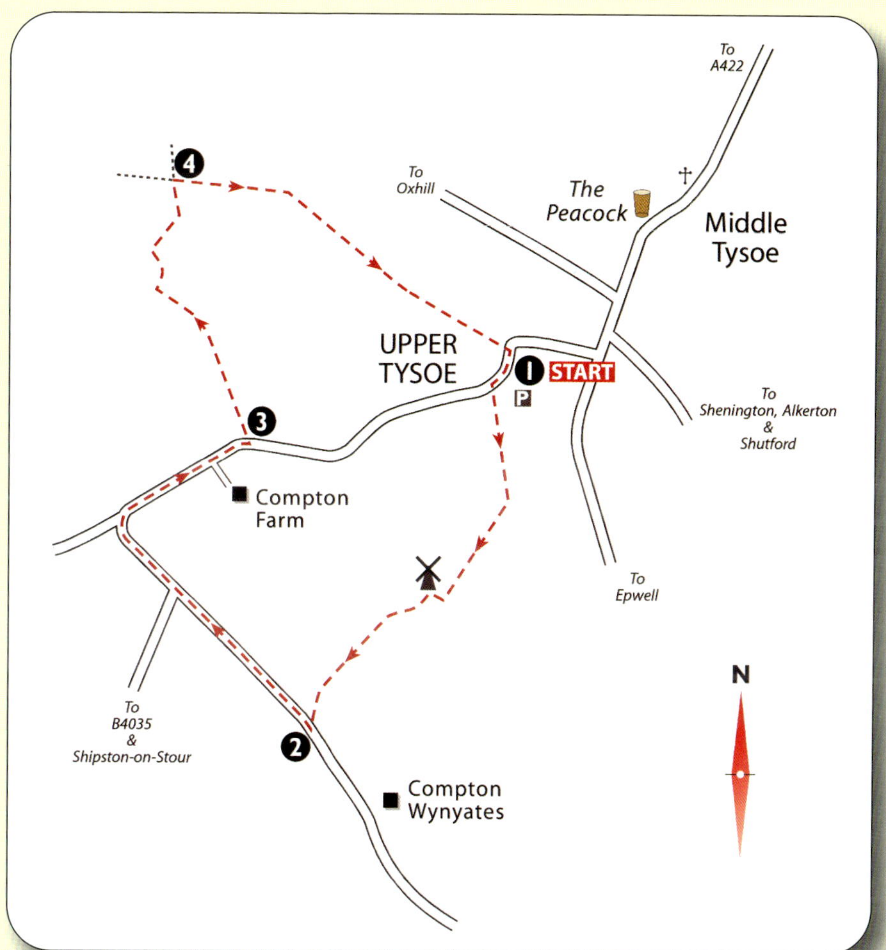

Introduction

Tysoe, in the Vale of the Red Horse, is divided into three parts: Lower, Middle and Upper. It is named after a horse which was cut into the hillside, but sadly ploughed up a couple of hundred years ago. The first part of the walk is quite a pull up to the top of Windmill Hill, but is well worth it for the wonderful views at the top. The route then passes the back of Compton Wynyates, a superb Tudor house, and drops down to cross fields and go through a wood. The varied countryside lends interest and makes this a most pleasant ramble through south Warwickshire.

Refreshments

The friendly **Peacock Inn** is in Main Street, Middle Tysoe. A relaxed atmosphere and a warm welcome make this a very pleasant village pub. Sandwiches and bar snacks, including scampi and chicken and chips, are served from 12.30 pm to 2.30 pm on Tuesday to Sunday and Chinese food is available in the evenings, either to eat in or to take away: 5 pm to 10.30 pm on Sunday to Thursday and 5 pm to 11 pm on Friday and Saturday. Telephone: 01295 680338.

THE WALK

Leave the lay-by and walk along the road for 40 yards, to a stile in the hedgerow on the left. Cross the stile and go straight across the field, up the hill, aiming to the left of the trees ahead. As the trees are approached, walk across to the left corner of the field to pass through a gap in the hedge, and carry on up the hill, with the hedge on the left. At the top left corner of the field, go left through the gap in the hedge and then immediately right to the windmill.

Pass to the left of the windmill and make for the stile in the hedge.

Compton Wynyates now comes into view, although from this aspect it doesn't present its best face. A Grade I listed building, it was constructed in the Tudor period over thirty years and has changed very little since. This beautiful house is owned and lived in by the Marquess of Northampton, but sadly is not open to the public.

Cross the stile and turn right to walk along with a fence on the right, and then a stone wall. At the next stile turn left and walk all the way down the hill to another stile. Go straight ahead along a wide track and cross a stile. The path is now between hedges. Cross the stile at the end and turn right onto the road.

Follow the road for about ½ mile, and keep straight ahead at the junction, signed '**Tysoe**'. After about ¼ mile the road bends right and goes up a gentle slope. Some 200 yards after passing the drive to **Compton Farm** on the right, turn left through a metal gate onto a footpath.

Keep the hedge and the stream on the left and pass through a gap into the next field. With the hedge still on the left, walk through the next field to a wooden gate. Some 160 yards after the gate, there is a gap in the hedge. Turn right to face the field, and set off on a line at about '10 o'clock'. (NB: There is no waymark at this point, but if you look into the field on the left you will see **Primrose Barn**, just to be sure you're in the right place.) As you get further up the field, aim for a point in the hedge where the high hedge meets a low hedge. Go through the gate and turn left to go through another gate.

The **Centenary Way** now joins the walk all the way back to **Tysoe**. Turn right and walk along the next field with the hedge on the right. At the corner of the field, look for a gate in the top hedge, 30 yards from the right field corner. Go through the gate and walk straight across the field to a metal gate and footbridge. Aim for the hedge corner 100 yards ahead on the right and then keep the field boundary on the right, heading for the far right corner of this field.

Turn right through the gap and immediately turn left, keeping the hedge on the left, to the next field boundary. Go through the gap in the hedge and then make for a gate about halfway along the hedge at the top of the field, amongst the trees. Walk straight ahead through the woods for about 150 yards, and then onto a grass track and eventually onto a gravel drive. Follow the drive to the road, turn right and walk along the road for about 150 yards, to return to the lay-by.

The windmill passed on the walk

PLACE OF INTEREST NEARBY

'About the most beautiful castle in all England … for sheer loveliness of the combination of water, woods and picturesque buildings.' So said Sir Charles Oman in 1898 of **Broughton Castle**. Privately owned by Lord and Lady Saye and Sele, the castle is to the south-west of Banbury. Open at Easter and then in the summer months. Telephone for details of days and times: 01295 276070.

19 Ilmington, Blackwell and Darlingscott

In the village of Blackwell

Distance 5 miles 2½ hours
Terrain A gentle ascent and descent at the beginning; otherwise level, on field paths and some country lanes **Map:** OS Explorer 205 (GR 212435)

How to get there

Take the A429 between junction 15 of the M40 and Moreton-in-Marsh. Approaching from the north, pass through the village of Halford and then take the right turn, signed to Armscote. Continue straight ahead at the next crossroads, go through Armscote and follow the signs to Ilmington. On entering the village, turn left at the T-junction into Front Street and drive as far as the Red Lion. **Parking:** On the street, near the Red Lion.

19 Ilmington, Blackwell and Darlingscott

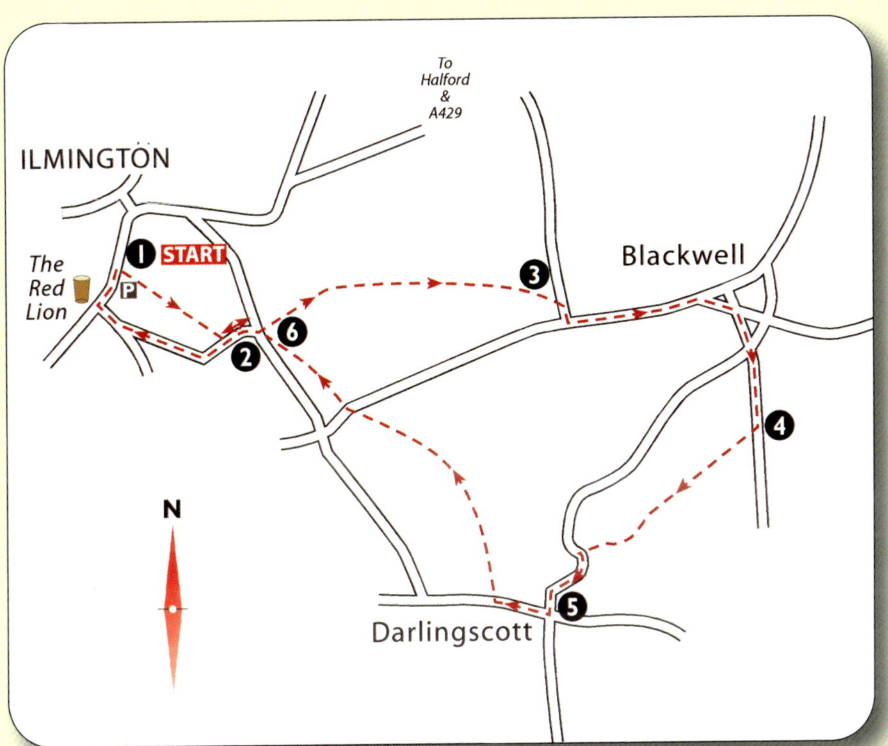

Introduction

Said to be the prettiest village in Warwickshire, Ilmington is popular with walkers. Footpaths radiate in all directions. This circuit goes through fields, farmland and two hamlets, Blackwell and Darlingscott. They are both sleepy backwaters, little changed over time, with attractive cottages and houses. Ilmington is a delightful place, with roads and lanes twisting here and there and rose-covered cottages built of Cotswold stone. There are far-reaching views from several points on the walk, and these are achieved without the usual slog associated with gaining height. The first part of the walk, as far as Blackwell, follows the Centenary Way.

Refreshments

A friendly welcome, good beer, a garden for sunny days and a wide choice of excellent food make the **Red Lion** in Ilmington's Front Street a good choice for post-walk refreshments. A varied menu includes tuna steaks, scampi, pies and sandwiches. Food is served from 12 noon to 2 pm and 5.30 pm to

8.45 pm on Monday to Friday, 12 noon to 8.45 pm on Saturday and 12 noon to 7 pm on Sunday. Telephone: 01608 682366.

THE WALK

Walk back down **Front Street** as far as **Lower Green**. Look for the footpath signed on the right immediately after the last cottage.

You will pass the village stocks, although they are in fact a modern replica.

Walk by the side of the house, through a gap in the hedge and over a stile. Continue up the field with the hedge on the left, to the brow, and then go diagonally across the field to the stile in the fence. Cross the next field, bearing slightly right, under the electricity wires.

Pause on the brow of the hill to enjoy the wonderful views from here, including Edgehill and Brailes Hill. The countryside rolls away for miles in a wide arc.

The path goes straight ahead, down the hill to the hedge ahead.

Walk through the gap in the hedge and turn left on the road. In 180 yards there is a T-junction. Go straight ahead, over the road, over the stile and onto the footpath, keeping the hedge on the left. The walk now passes through three fields, keeping the hedge on the left. Towards the end of the third field, the path leaves the hedge and crosses the field to the far boundary, going under electricity wires. Cross the stile by the willow tree and walk straight across the field to the next stile. Continue straight ahead, and then follow the path as it turns slightly to the right to a stile.

Cross the stile and turn right on the country road to the T-junction, and then left to **Blackwell**, where the walk leaves the **Centenary Way**. Take the right fork to enter the village.

Stay for a moment to savour the quiet. Here houses surround the little village green, quiet country roads meander along and it is easy to imagine how life was lived a century or more ago.

Follow the road and turn right at the road intersection. At the next crossroads go straight across, signed to Shipston and Moreton.

After 300 yards, turn right into a field and head diagonally left across it, under some electricity wires, slightly to the right of the

The Howard Arms in Ilmington

pylon in the field. Cross the stile in the field corner.

Warwickshire is one of the few counties where the ancient ridge and furrow system of agriculture still remains. The field you are about to enter is a good example.

Walk ahead and pass through a field gate to the left of a broken stile. Go straight ahead through the next field, cross a stile and continue on the same line. Towards the far side of the field a hedgerow begins. Keep it on the right for 50 yards, following the path as it turns to the left, and in 10 yards look carefully for a stile in the hedge. The footpath now passes between wooden fences to another stile and emerges onto a lane. Turn left and follow the road into **Darlingscott**.

Darlingscott is another sleepy village, in the midst of farming country. Little interrupts the tranquillity.

At the crossroads turn right, signed 'Ilmington 2 miles'. After 200 yards, turn right down **Potter's Lane**.

There is a useful bench on the corner here, a good place for a rest and refreshment.

Keep straight ahead, past all the houses, to cross a wooden footbridge and a stile and enter a field. Head straight ahead over the field to the stile in the opposite boundary. Cross the stile and continue straight ahead. At the field corner bear slightly left to go through another field to a stile in a hedge.

Now set your path diagonally across the next field, following the direction of the waymarked sign on the stile, aiming for a gap in the hedge on the opposite boundary. Cross the stile in the hedge, go straight over the road and into the next field. Go almost straight across the field, again following the direction of the waymarked arrow. Pass through the gap in the hedge and walk straight across the next field. At the next boundary, go diagonally across to the far left of the field to emerge onto the road by a T-junction.

Go straight ahead, signed to **Ilmington**, and walk back along the road to the village. If you have time, take a wander around and enjoy the pathways that run between the cottages, the attractive gardens and the rich mellow Cotswold stone.

PLACES OF INTEREST NEARBY

To the west of Ilmington, just over the border in Gloucestershire, is **Kiftsgate Court Garden**. Kiftsgate is a series of interconnecting gardens, each with its own character. Telephone: 01386 438777.

Hidcote Manor Garden is a National Trust property and one of the country's great gardens. It is famous for its unusual shrubs and trees, and has wonderful herbaceous borders. Telephone: 01386 438333.

20 Cherington

Cherington

Distance 3 miles 1½ hours
Terrain A fairly steep ascent and descent with some level walking; mainly field paths, and a small amount of road in the village
Map: OS Explorer OL45 (GR 293368)

How to get there

Follow the A3400, south from Shipston-on-Stour for a little less than 3 miles. Turn left at the sign for Cherington. This is the third turning left after leaving Shipston-on-Stour. In a little less than 2 miles, the road enters the village. Follow it through the village and take the first left, pass the church, then take the first right. The Cherington Arms is along here on the left. **Parking:** In the pub car park if you are eating here (please ask the landlord). Otherwise continue on and park where the road becomes wider.

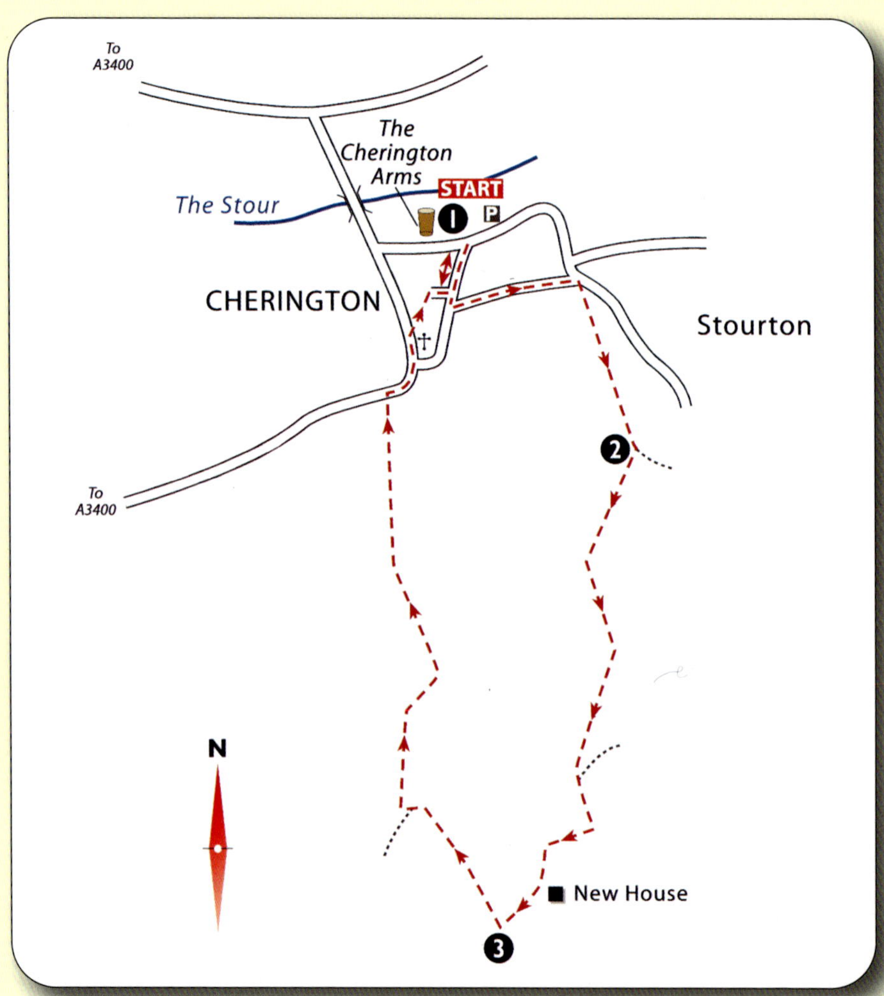

Introduction

The main features of this walk are the delightful countryside and extensive views. Cherington is on the northern boundary of the Cotswolds, and many of the houses are built of the local golden stone. Cherington joins seamlessly to its neighbour Stourton and together the two villages are a delight to walk round, their gardens brimming with flowers in the summer months. This is also farming country, with many of the fields given over to cereal crops. Up on the top, one is far from everyday busy life; therapy for the soul indeed.

This is a short walk, with a steep ascent, but well worth the effort for the panoramic views in all directions.

Refreshments

The **Cherington Arms** is a friendly country pub with a large dining room, and an attractive garden leading down to the River Stour. There is a good choice of bar snacks, meals and sandwiches. Food is served on Monday 12 noon to 2 pm; Tuesday to Thursday 12 noon to 2 pm and 7 pm to 9 pm; Friday 12 noon to 2 pm and 7 pm to 9.30 pm; Saturday and Sunday 12 noon to 2.30 pm and 7 pm to 9.30 pm (9 pm on Sunday). Telephone: 01608 686233.

THE WALK

From the **Cherington Arms**, continue ahead, with the pub on the left. Turn right along **Featherbed Lane** and, in about 60 yards, take the waymarked footpath on the left next to a metal gate. Follow the path, with a fence on the left and a hedge on the right, as it goes gently uphill to join a road. Turn left on the road and look for the telephone box (a modern type) set back in the hedge, in a couple of hundred yards. Turn right just after the phone box, and walk along a wide track. The path soon narrows and passes between trees. Cross the stile at the end into a field and walk along it with the boundary on the left. Cross the stile in the field corner and continue ahead, with the hedge still on the left, to the next field corner.

Go through the gate and turn 45° right, heading up the hill to a distant gap in the trees on the rise at the far end of the field. Go straight ahead keeping the woods, and then a hedge, on the left, to cross a stile in the top left corner. Follow the path diagonally as it goes steeply up the field to the top right corner.

Pause a moment to regain your breath and enjoy the stunning views.

Keep straight ahead through the gap in the hedge and continue uphill with the hedge on the left. Cross a stile and continue at 45° as directed by the waymarker to the top right corner of the field. Continue upwards again with the hedge on the left to the gap in the far hedge. Turn right, keeping the hedge on the right. At the end of the hedge, the path curves left to the corner of a wood. Turn right and follow the wire fence, passing a large, newly-built house on the left, to the hedge on the far side of the field.

③

Turn right at the hedge and, keeping the hedge on the left, walk to a metal gate. Continue straight ahead, downhill to the next field corner. Go through the metal gate slightly to the left of the field corner. Follow the path with the hedge on the left for almost ¼ mile. Where the field dips, turn left through a waymarked gap.

There are some lovely views of the village and the church from here.

Follow the path with the hedge on the right. The hedge changes to the left at the next field boundary. Head on down all the way towards **Cherington**. The path widens as it enters the village, and joins the road opposite a post box. Turn right on the road, and, just after the bend, turn left at the junction, signed 'Cherington Arms'. After 60 yards, turn right into the churchyard, and follow the grassy path, which passes round the left of the church. At the end of the path is a metal gate into a field. Bear right diagonally across the field, aiming just to the right of a double telegraph pole.

This field is an excellent example of ridge and furrow.

Cross over the stile and turn right along the road. At the end turn left into **Featherbed Lane** and then left again to return to the **Cherington Arms**.

PLACE OF INTEREST NEARBY

The **Rollright Stones** near Long Compton, reached to the south of Cherington along the A3400, are a Neolithic stone circle built for ceremonies, dating from around 2,000 BC. Many folk stories are told about its origin, but the most popular one is that the king and his men were passing by when they met a witch. The witch told the king: 'If Long Compton thou canst see, King of England thou shalt be.' The king was told to take seven steps forward, but he couldn't see Long Compton, so the witch turned him and his men into stone. The stone circle represents the king's men, the king stands on his own some distance away, and the Whispering Knights are in a further corner, said to be plotting against the king. Open every day, during daylight.